40 YEARS OF THE COUNTRYSIDE EDUCATION TRUST AT BEAULIEU IN THE NEW FOREST

An environmentally friendly book printed and bound in England by www.printondemand-worldwide.com

Mixed Sources
Product group from well-managed
forests, and other controlled sources
www.fsc.org Cert no. TT-COC-002641
© 1996 Forest Stewardship Council

PEFC Certified
This product is
from sustainably
managed forests
and controlled
sources
www.pefc.org
PEFC/16-33-415

This book is made entirely of chain-of-custody materials

FastPrint
Publishing

www.fast-print.net/store.php

First published 2015 by
FASTPRINT PUBLISHING
Peterborough, England.

Contents

Acknowledgements:

Pictures provided by CET & Motor Museum archives, Rick Withers, David Quoroll, Mike & Louise Shrubsole and Steve & Rosalyn Reed. Many thanks to all the people who have helped with the production of this book. Special thanks to Steve Barnard, Ken and Ann Matthews and Steve Reed without whom this book would not have been completed.

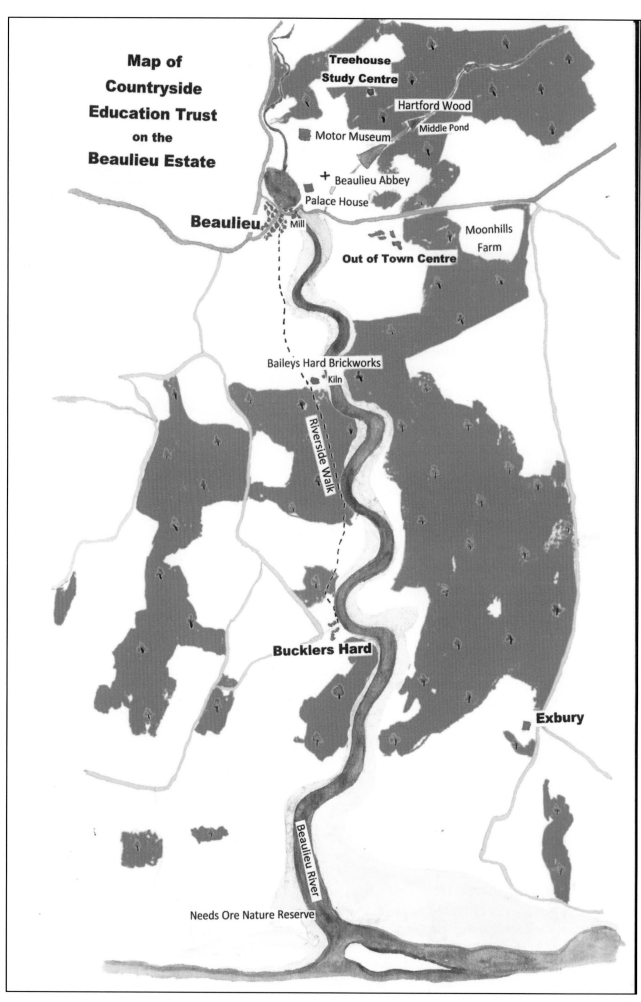

Map of
Countryside
Education Trust
on the
Beaulieu Estate

Treehouse
Study Centre

Hartford Wood

Middle Pond

Motor Museum

Beaulieu Abbey

Palace House

Beaulieu

Mill

Moonhills
Farm

Out of Town Centre

Baileys Hard Brickworks

Kiln

Riverside Walk

Bucklers Hard

Exbury

Beaulieu River

Needs Ore Nature Reserve

Foreword

Forty years ago, the idea that children – and others – needed to learn about the countryside, and where food came from, was a new one. It took the vision of my father Lord Montagu, television personality Jack Hargreaves and Beaulieu's first Head of Education Graham Carter to do something about it by establishing centres on the Beaulieu Estate.

Today there are a number organisations concerned with countryside education, several with names similar to our own, but in 1975, we were the first! This comprehensive account illustrates just how much dedication, hard work and fundraising has been required to get the Countryside Education Trust established with the facilities and track record it has today. In our first forty years, we have catered for over 300,000 children on day visits, over 45,000 on residential weeks and around 80,000 adults and children from the local community. We have pushed the boundaries of environmental education and brought many disadvantaged urban people into the countryside for the first time.

I commend Rosalyn Reed for her work in putting this history together. She was the best placed person to do it, as she was there for most of it! For those involved with the Countryside Education Trust of today, and possibly others concerned with education and the environment, this book is for you. One can always learn from history!

Honorable Ralph Montagu

History of the Countryside Education Trust

Introduction

Before the industrial revolution almost everybody was part of the countryside. They lived and worked there. Towns and cities were small and still served as hubs for the majority of the population who lived on the land. By the mid 1940s, with mechanisation and modern practices, and the rapid increase in population, towns and cities had grown apart from the countryside and people felt excluded. Land owners had become used to their land being their own private property and many were unwilling to give access to those who were not employed on their estates. Some people became angry that such large areas of the country were owned by a relatively few people and they were not allowed any access to it. In response to this there were demonstrations and acts of mass trespass and there was real conflict.

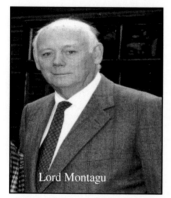

In 1949 the National Parks and Access to the Countryside Act was passed and this opened the way for agreements with landowners to ensure increased access to the countryside was made available. Throughout the 1950's and early 1960s there was a steady increase in affluence and mobility. This made it much easier for people who lived in towns and cities to get out into the countryside and they wanted somewhere to go. At the same time, a number of far seeing and innovative owners opened their homes and parts of their estates to paying visitors. This helped to raise funds to maintain the estates, which was becoming an increasing challenge, and also provided the destinations that people craved.

Lord Montagu

Lord Montagu was one of the first landowners to open his home in this way. In 1952 Palace House became a visitor destination, and people loved it. They came in their droves to see Palace House and the vintage cars that had become a real feature there. They also visited the abbey buildings and ruins, the villages of Beaulieu and Buckler's Hard, and the woods, farmland and open forest. By 1962 there were over 400,000 paying visitors to the estate each year, plus all those who just visited the countryside around, and it was becoming a problem. Many visitors who ventured onto the farmland and into the woods on the estate did not seem to be aware that they could be in danger from animals, machinery or other rural industry. Nor were they mindful of the fact that they could do harm to the livelihood of those who lived and worked in the country. By their sheer numbers the people could actually destroy the environment they wanted to enjoy. Their cars were an even greater problem, so access needed to be managed very carefully if the needs of visitors, the resident population and the environment were all to be taken into consideration. There needed to be a plan.

Lord Montagu and his Agent, Brian Hubbard, travelled to many places in the world broadening their knowledge of how others were dealing with the growing pressure from people of all ages to visit and enjoy places of great beauty, and interest. They were very impressed by the professional attitude and approach which prevailed in North America and certain places in Western Europe, and they made particular study of

Palace House (left)
Beaulieu Abbey Church
(right)
The Cloisters (below)

the educational uses of the countryside and places of special interest. In 1966 Lord Montagu commissioned Elizabeth Chesterton, a landscape planner, to draw up a Conservation Plan to ensure the long-term enhancement and survival of the Beaulieu Estate and address the problems caused by large numbers of visitors. The plan was adopted in principle by Hampshire County Council as the basis of county planning policy for the area and the scene was set for these ideas to be put in motion.

In 1971/72 big changes came about in Beaulieu. A by-pass was built around the village, large new car parks were laid, and a new building was constructed to house the ever growing collection of vintage cars and motoring memorabilia. The John Montagu Building was erected to provide offices for staff, plus an entrance hall and shop to provide access and facilities for visitors. To ensure the future of the collection of cars the Motor Museum Trust was set up and a new building erected to house it. Developments were also going on at Bucklers Hard to improve parking and preserve the little village for all to enjoy.

Now the way was clear for an exciting and inclusive educational service to be established. This would give people of all ages an opportunity to learn about the rich history of the Beaulieu Estate, and gain access in a safe, enjoyable and informative way to all areas of the countryside.

Lord Montagu at
Bucklers Hard (left)
Palace House (below)

Chapter 1

Education is Established

Early in 1972 an advertisement was placed in The Times for the position of Education Officer. He/she would have the task of developing the educational potential of the whole of the Beaulieu Estate. At the same time access was to be made available to open country, rivers, woodlands and agricultural land. Children and young people were to be given particular attention so that 'days out' in the countryside were to be educational as well as enjoyable.

In answer to the advertisement over 250 people applied for the job of Education Officer, and Ken Robinson, Managing Director, was charged with the task of selecting the best person for the job. Eventually it was down to the last two people and they were each invited to attend a weekend selection procedure. They were given accommodation, with their wives, at the Master Builder's House Hotel at Buckler's Hard and met by Ken and Christine Robinson, and Brian and Philippa Hubbard for an enjoyable but anxious time. Finally the appointment was made and Graham Carter became the first Beaulieu Education Officer.

Graham Carter

Graham was a young science teacher in his early 30s, with a degree in environmental sciences. He had been teaching in Hackney in North London and already shown great flare in his ability to engage young people. At his post at Hackney Free and Parochial School he had seen the potential for using not only his classroom, but the roof of the science block where he worked. There he had established, with his pupils, gardens, a greenhouse, an aviary, an aquarium and many other teaching aids. He was also appointed second in command at the North London Science Centre where many teachers had benefited from his advice and encouragement, certainly a worthy applicant for the challenge presented by the work on the Beaulieu Estate.

A cottage in the centre of the Motor Museum grounds was made available, and Graham moved to Beaulieu with his wife and young family. It was a traditional Victorian cottage with very limited amenities. The tiny bathroom was off the kitchen and fitted in under the stairs. Getting in and out of the bath could result in a nasty bump on the head if extreme care was not taken. There was no such thing as central heating or insulation and the kitchen was really basic, but that was all part of the challenge. He started work on 1st April 1972. In later years he often said that he wondered if he was indeed an April Fool.

The task he had undertaken was daunting. First he had to acquaint himself with the workings of the estate and get to know the people who worked there. The 8,000 acres of the estate included the villages of Beaulieu and Buckler's Hard, 2,000 acres of woodland, 4,000 acres of farmland, eight miles of Beaulieu river and four miles of foreshore. In addition there was Palace House, Lord Montagu's family home, Beaulieu Abbey and now the National Motor Museum.

National Motor Museum, Beaulieu

Graham Carter worked with Lord Montagu, Brian Hubbard, Ken Robinson, Jeremy Stanley Smith and a well known television presenter, Jack Hargreaves, and many others, to produce a document outlining the enormous educational potential of the estate. This included the provision of day visitor facilities at the Motor Museum and Bucklers Hard. The brickworks at Baileys Hard also offered a potential site and there was farming interest that could be based at Park Farm. A centre in Hartford Wood would allow visitors to experience and learn about the woodland environment and fresh water ecology, and there would be access to the nature reserve at Needs Ore. Also planned was a residential centre so young people from inner cities, aged 8 – 13 could spend more time in the countryside. All these provisions would give areas and covered spaces where students of all ages could gain access, free of charge, to the range of habitats, features and facilities available throughout the estate.

The next thing required were sources of income to fund this work. Everyone set to work to find people who might become involved and contribute to this valuable initiative. Graham went back to those he knew at ILEA, approached industries and investigated the many charitable Trusts who made funds available for educational work. Jack Hargreaves looked to Southern TV and sought funds there. Lord Montagu had many

contacts and influential people he could approach for support, so requests went out in all directions. However, it soon became clear that, if money was to be obtained from many of these sources, the educational work had to be established as a charity, so Graham set to work to find a way of registering it as such.

The Charity Commission seemed to have some difficulty at first in understanding the nature of this educational initiative. It didn't quite fit in to any of their categories and much work had to be done to ensure that the format of the application was just right. Suitable places had to be chosen for the day visitor facilities, and a site had to be made available for a residential centre. A hut that had served as an amusement arcade on the motor museum site was made available for day visitors there, and started to function for that purpose, providing exciting educational days for schools. Meanwhile a site on Home Farm was identified as the most suitable place for the residential centre to be established. At this stage the initiative was called the Beaulieu Education Department.

The objectives of the newly established Beaulieu Education Department were defined as follows:

a) To provide additional access to the countryside for young people in organised parties.
b) To develop the full educational potential of the Beaulieu Manor Estate.
c) To provide such facilities as may be necessary to enable this development to proceed.
d) To make these facilities available without charge to any group or individual who may derive benefit from their use.
e) To plan educational services in such a way that they are always compatible with plans for the conservation of the Estate and the New Forest.

COUNTRYSIDE EDUCATION TRUST

1975 - 76

The Countryside Education Trust was registered as a charity in May 1975. Graham Carter had already done a lot of work since his appointment as Education Officer in 1972, but with the establishment of the CET as a charity the work could move on with much greater focus.

The first meeting of the Founder Trustees was held on 24th June 1975, followed by a meeting of the whole Board of Trustees on 28th July 1975. The Board of Trustees was a truly impressive body. Represented within it were landowners, a television personality, men from business and industry, people from schools and education, and a member of the local council. Also present at the meetings were staff of the Motor Museum and the Beaulieu Estate and the Director of the Countryside Education Trust.

At the first meeting of the Trustees it was important to look at what had already been done and consider how the organisation should proceed.

The projects that had been established were already considerable, and there were many additional ideas of ways in which the estate could be opened up for educational activities. Education at the Motor Museum and Buckler's Hard had moved on apace. Educational services had been made available to all visiting school groups, and nearly half of them had taken advantage of the new services on offer.

A Woodland Walk had been established within Hartford Wood with paths laid out and surfaced ready for use. This was made available to people using the Motor Museum at a small charge, but so far, there had been little interest shown by the general public. It was used, however, by visiting school groups and was of great educational value.

A Riverside Walk had been created running from the Montagu Arms at Beaulieu, to Buckler's Hard. This ran passed the Brickworks at Bailey's Hard and on through the woodland at Keeping Copse with wonderful views of the Beaulieu Estuary.

A trail had been set up at Park Farm so that people could have access to the farmland and could see and enjoy the animals there. Many groups of children had already visited the farm and learnt about farming methods, land use and animal husbandry.

The Tide Mill in Beaulieu village was identified as a place where a craft museum could be set up. Roy Bowman, a countryman with much experience of country life and craft, had a large collection of tools, machinery and other artefacts associated with country crafts, and he was willing to make these available to the CET. These would make an impressive display within the Tide Mill. In addition, there could be a Craft Shop and the Beaulieu Weavers could be encouraged to make the mill their headquarters which would give life and interest to the museum.

The Needs Ore Bird Sanctuary, at the mouth of the Beaulieu River, was another important area. Bird hides could be built, and educational groups could learn about the importance of the estuary and coastal salt marshes to both resident and migrating birds. They could also study coastal features and habitats there. Discussions were going on with the Nature Conservancy Council to establish a National Nature Reserve along a large part of the North Solent shore and Needs Ore would be a significant part of this.

It had also been decided that a residential centre for children and young people should be established on the Beaulieu estate, and that the land at Home Farm would be the most appropriate site.

There were big plans and the biggest problem would be raising sufficient funds to support this ambitious work. A grant of £3000 was received from IBM, another £3000 from Montagu Ventures Ltd. and £150 from Whitbread, but Graham reported early in 1976 that he had 75 letters of refusal, another 40 people had not replied, and only 7 donations had resulted from his fundraising efforts. Educational materials, and booklets and leaflets on Buckler's Hard, Riverside Walk and Need's Ore brought in some income, but raising funds was a real struggle. However, there was enormous determination that the work should go on and the numbers of groups using the educational services already developed was increasing all the time.

Raising the Funds

The expertise gained by Graham by that time was considerable, and it was suggested by Lord Sandford that another way of raising funds would be to market Graham's expertise. This could be offered to Local Education Authorities, the owners of Historic Houses and even tenant farmers. A new publicity folder had been created detailing all the educational activities and materials on offer. This was circulated to schools, environmental advisers, teachers' centres, and tour operators who organised school trips throughout the south of England. The publicity received an immediate response from teachers, and four Open Days were organised in order to show them all the facilities available through the CET. So many teachers responded that even these four were not enough to meet the demand.

The Historic Houses Association quickly saw the potential of using Graham's expertise and appointed him as Education Advisory Officer. This was financed by a grant of £2,500 from the Department of the Environment, which greatly helped CET funds. As the Historic Housing Association had designated 1977 as Heritage Education Year there was clearly going to be much work to do, and before the end of 1976 there had been 20 requests from Historic Houses for Graham to make a personal visit to discuss possible educational programmes.

The Council of Europe was also keen to use Graham's services to prepare a questionnaire for member countries on Environmental Education. He was able to sign a contract with them from 1st January 1977 for which £600 would be paid into Trust funds. He was also asked to organise a conference for the Council of Europe to take place in the UK in July 1977.

All this activity away from Beaulieu would severely limit Graham's time in developing the educational programme on the estate. However, the Government had set up a 'Job Creation Programme' under the Manpower Services Commission, and a successful application provided a team of three teachers and a graphic designer to work for the Trust. They would be employed from 1st August 1976 for 13 months for which the Trust would receive £11,500 for staff and equipment from the MSC. Graham appointed the staff and they quickly got to work producing educational packs for the woodland, Palace House, Beaulieu Abbey and the National Motor Museum. They were also involved in planning the future educational programme, so they soon became a great asset to the Trust. As the Job Creation Programme was to continue into the following year, Graham immediately applied again for another team to start as soon as the first one finished.

It seems impossible to imagine how Graham fitted in all the work in those early years – continuous fundraising activities, helping with the planning of the new residential centre, identifying the educational potential of all the different sites, producing leaflets and brochures, advertising for, recruiting and supervising staff, teaching visiting groups and dashing around this country and Europe. The workload was enormous, but support came from many areas.

Graham's wife, Margaret, and his two children, Jane and David, were a great help. The children were at junior school at this time, so in holidays and at weekends they would often be seen with their mother helping to clear paths and set up trails. Margaret would also help with administration tasks, putting up posters and helping with the many fundraising events.

Fiona, Lady Montagu became a great ally. She and Graham shared many interests. She was just as passionate about education as he was and would do anything in her power to help fund or promote the work. There is even a story of her meeting a millionaire of her acquaintance on the beach one day, and persuading him there and then to give a large donation to the work of the Countryside Education Trust.

Lady Montagu and Graham also shared an interest in amateur dramatics. They had both been involved in different productions of Wind in the Willows in their youth and had a matching love of the absurd character of Toad of Toad Hall. When things were going especially badly and there seemed no way forward, they would raise their spirits by quoting Toad's words "Oh bliss, oh rapture, oh poop-poop!" This usually produced a laugh and reduced the tension so that they could carry on. Lady Montagu set up a fundraising committee with the help of a friend, Jane Adley. This involved over 20 ladies who were interested in education including Lady Montagu's mother Mrs Herbert.

Mrs Herbert was a wonderful support and would do anything to help with projects that would enable her daughter to fulfil her many commitments or promote the work of the CET. She looked after Jonathan, the baby son of Lord and Lady Montagu, whenever she was needed. She helped with all manner of fundraising events including setting up the CET Christmas Fair held annually in Palace House. She organised stalls, sent out invitations to the great and the good, advertised it and carried out many of the practical tasks required to stage this prestigious event. It became one of the main fundraising attractions raising tens of thousands of pounds each year for the Trust.

Other fundraising events included: cooking demonstrations, fashion shows, bridge days, concerts, banquets, open houses and gardens, talks, good second hand clothes sales and many more. These have continued to be run by the fundraising committee inspired and directed by the boundless enthusiasm of Lady Montagu.

In the autumn of 1976 it was realised that the residential centre, to be known as the Out of Town Centre, needed to become a separate organisation from the Countryside Education Trust as the volume of work required and the organisation of the new centre could no longer be managed in the same way as the other educational initiatives.

Victorian buildings at the Home Farm site later to be the Out of Town Centre

Royal Kent School,
Oakshade road,
Oxshott,
Surrey
KT22 OLE.
Monday 10th october

Dear Beaulieu,

I am writing this letter to say thank you for all the incredible activities all of them were amazing (except for the table laying) allthough that wasn't that bad. My favourite activities were the cattle and goat's and the palace walk. I liked doing cattle and goats because the cattle liked the food off your hand and they were realy soft. I also liked the milking the goats because I never knew it was so fun. I liked the palace walk and it was interesting to know how hard it must of been for a victorian child. I just want to say another massive thank you for all the brilliant activities and of course the food. I could never thank you enough enough.

Love from Luca

Chapter 2

The Out of Town Centre Begins

The residential centre based on Home Farm was the brain child of the well known television presenter Jack Hargreaves. He was born in London, although his main home was in Huddersfield in West Yorkshire. He was the son of a successful business man in the woollen industry so his home life was relatively well-to-do but, he was not a very happy child. He was rather rebellious and frequently at odds with his father causing him great concern. His life was very urban and he went to public school from quite an early age, which didn't seem to suit him at all well. He became a real problem to his parents, but his mother saw that he had a great interest in the countryside, which she felt should be nurtured and encouraged.

Jack Hargreaves

They had a family friend who was a south country farmer and she arranged for Jack to go and stay with him during one of his school holidays. This was just what Jack needed. He seemed to come alive on the farm and in contrast to his difficult behaviour at home he settled there and made great friends with the farmer and his family. When his parents found he was happier there, many further holidays were arranged until the farm became more home to him than his own family house.

It was on the farm that he learnt many of the skills of farming. These included milking, caring for the animals, ploughing, shepherding, shooting and fishing. He learnt to set traps and nets to catch rabbits, and to hunt with a ferret and a gun. He also learnt to respect the life of the countryside. He became so interested in countryside ways that he read widely on all aspects of the subject until he became something of an expert on country matters.

Although he hated school he was able to get good results and went on to university where he studied veterinary science. However, his studies were cut short when his father's business interests took a serious down turn and he was thrust into the world of work. His career took him towards work in the media, first with the press and radio and later in television.

On 6th July 1960 he became the presenter of the much loved television programme 'Out of Town'. This gave Jack the opportunity to use his extensive knowledge and love of the countryside, and the programme brought countryside matters and concerns to the very hearts of his viewers. Although he worked and made the programmes for Southern Television, they became popular all over the country and he became famous and well loved by all who enjoyed them.

During the 1950s and 60s his interests brought him in touch with the shoot on the Beaulieu Estate where he became a member. He became well known to Lord Montagu and when the idea of opening up the Beaulieu Estate for countryside education was discussed he was very enthusiastic. His experience on the farm in his youth had made such an impact on him that he felt that other young people should be given the opportunity of staying on a farm and experiencing country life. It was during their discussions that the idea of establishing a residential centre on the Beaulieu Estate was born.

The land on Home Farm was an ideal site. The lower part of the site was close to the road that ran down the hill to the village. It had been used as a clay pit for many years so the sheltered hollow this provided would be an ideal spot for the residential and farm buildings. The higher land had fields running down to the Beaulieu River estuary with a magnificent view, and enough space to establish a small mixed farm.

There was much discussion about what the residential facility should be called, but Jack was never in doubt. It would be known as The Out of Town Centre and made available for urban children aged 8 – 13 years to receive an introduction to the life of the countryside.

Initially the Out of Town Centre was part of the Countryside Education Trust. However, the residential centre needed to be run in a rather different way in order for funds to be raised and for it to receive the support it needed, so a separate management committee was set up in 1976. This consisted of Jack Hargreaves, one of the Founder Trustees, Graham Carter, Director of the Countryside Education Trust, and Jeremy Stanley Smith, Land Agent for the Beaulieu Estate who would be responsible for the implementation of the project.

Much work had to be done. A lease had to be drawn up by the Estate for the land to be used for the Out of Town Centre. A new entrance to the road had to be established with the agreement of the local authority, and most pressing of all, funds of an estimated £160,000 had to be obtained.

After much discussion Graham was able to obtain a capital sum of £70,000 from ILEA (the Inner London Education Authority), with an additional £23,000 for running costs. This was then matched by Southern Television. It was agreed with ILEA that the residential centre be run as a limited company under separate management, which became known as the Out of Town Country Pursuits Centre Ltd and it was registered as an independent charity, the Out of Town Trust. Although there was still much co-operation, and some educational services were provided by the CET, the residential centre and farm was now a separate organisation. A separate Governing Committee was set up and the two organisations gradually drew apart.

Rear of Out of Town Centre

13

Establishment of the Out of Town Centre

A committee was set up in 1978 to oversee the running of the Out of Town Centre. It was chaired by Mr George Gould, President of the Veterinary Society. A 66 year lease was agreed with the Beaulieu Estate for land totalling 60 acres, and No 1 Home Farm Cottages and No 1 The Studio were obtained to house a farmer and a warden with their families. The building of the residential centre started in January 1979 and there were high hopes that it would be completed and ready for occupation within the year.

Charlie Knight

In April 1979 Charlie and Elaine Knight were appointed as farmer and his wife to work together as a team to provide a range of learning activities on the farm. The programme would also include visits to large scale specialised farming enterprises, farm sales and cattle markets, and the Countryside Education Trust would provide other countryside and environmental activities. A tractor and trailer and other farm machinery and tools were bought or donated to the charity, and plans were drawn up of suitable farm buildings that would house the animals. The stock included beef and dairy cattle, goats, pigs, poultry, geese and sheep, so a good range of animals to give the young visitors a really wide experience. A small pick up van was also bought for farm transport.

Elaine Knight teaching a group of children

It was now time to obtain the staff needed for the residential centre. An advertisement was placed for a warden/teacher to be appointed, and Mr David Robinson took up the position in September 1979. The job of executive secretary was then advertised and Mrs Suzan Portlock was appointed. Office accommodation was provided at Palace House initially until the centre was ready.

In December there was concern that the revenue budget had been exceeded and more funds were needed to complete the building of the residential centre. Southern Television agreed to provide a further £25,000 and Hampshire County Council £5,000 to help with the cost of construction. The centre was ready for occupation by 15th January 1980 and the first group arrived from Woodberry Down School on 25th February. The charge for each child was £48.75 for a five day visit or £55 for seven days. This required that the centre was occupied by 32 children each week for 40 weeks each year if the books were to balance.

Dave Robinson

David Robinson prepared a detailed programme of activities that might be undertaken by the children. They would be involved in practical activities, observation and investigation. Much of their work would be on-site, but for off-site activities transport would be needed. Lord Montagu approached the Ford Motor Company who offered to supply a new minibus with automatic transmission at a good discount. This was accepted, and it was delivered in time for the arrival of the first group.

Mrs H Blake was appointed as Cook/Housekeeper. She was offered a temporary position for the term until April in order to minimise cost. As she lived locally, she was prepared to be on call in case of emergency, which was a real benefit.

Work was started on the farm buildings in February. They had been rather delayed by difficulty in obtaining planning consent. Then further delays were experienced when the weather was exceptionally wet in March and problems were encountered during the construction. This meant that smaller numbers of animals could be kept and teaching programmes had to be adapted until the work was completed.

Local people were invited to visit the new centre on 10th May so that they could feel part of this new venture and see what was happening on their doorstep. The centre was officially opened on 25th April by Lord Malmesbury with an opening ceremony and lunch at the Domus. Local dignitaries, those who were involved in setting up the centre, including representatives from Southern Television and ILEA, the Governors, the Press and County Education Officers from a wide area, all took part. After lunch they were transported by

coach to the Out of Town Centre to see the residential centre and farm. It was a great event and a sundial given by Southern Television was unveiled to mark the occasion.

20 groups from ILEA schools stayed at the centre in 1980. There were also schools from Berkshire (8) East Sussex (3) and Dorset (1). This made a total of 32 weeks booked, which was very encouraging.

The daily routine was as follows: rise at 7.30am, half the group would go out and feed animals while the other half did chores inside such as setting the tables for breakfast, which was at 8.30. At 9.30am they were briefed on the day's activities which were divided into morning and afternoon sessions. These continued until the children returned to the centre in time to get ready for the evening meal at about 5pm. Groups then went out to do animal feeding, or stayed to do chores within the hostel. Evening activities were led by the school staff.

A maximum 32 children stayed at the centre each week. Most of the time, they were divided into two groups. One group was taken off-site, while the other was occupied around the site or within the local area. A number of options were offered to the schools. These included: a general study of the farm, working on the farm, feeding and tending the animals; a visit to the New Forest, a cattle market, or other farms in the area; a river, coast or woodland study. Both children and school staff were very enthusiastic about their stay.

Funding the work continued to present problems and a Finance Committee was set up to address these. There was a considerable deficit which needed to be

15

covered and further expenditure was required. It was estimated that £100,000 to £200,000 was needed at that time, so it was no small task that the Committee was taking on. It was also necessary to raise charges, and a new rate of £64 per 5 day visit and £68.50 for a 6 day visit was suggested. This should start at the end of March 1981.

The Out of Town Centre and the Countryside Education Trust continued to work closely together. Funds raised by the OTC Fundraising Committee were to be divided between the two charities as the CET provided support and facilities to the OTC. The CET Countryside Education Officer, Mrs Kate Glegg who was appointed to the staff of the CET on 1st June 1980, was teaching OTC groups for two days each week and there were many projects planned that would be of benefit to both charities.

Housing presented problems at this time as No 1 The Studio, where the Warden and his family were living, was in a very poor condition. The roof leaked, the walls were damp, and there were many other problems with it. Staff of the Beaulieu Estate were asked to put in hand the necessary repairs to the fabric of the building so that the Governors of the OTC could improve the interior of the house.

Work continued on the farm. The Beaulieu Estate provided a hen house, which made it possible to purchase and install the first flock of laying hens. The eggs would be used in the residential centre. Ducks and geese were soon seen roaming freely in the farmyard. Vegetables were grown for the centre. Goats became an interesting addition and the children were shown how to milk them. A herd of cattle was bought and soon young ones were born so increasing the herd. Pigs were also obtained and the resulting piglets were raised

and sold at a profit. They were a great favourite with the children. Wheat, barley and oats were grown providing straw for animal bedding, and hay was cut for feed. The children were involved in every aspect of the farming and loved the whole experience.

16

Approaches were made to Berkshire, Hampshire, East
Sussex, Kent, Surrey and Dorset education departments
in order to try and fill the empty weeks in the residential
centre during the term time. Their response was very
disappointing and none of them took up the opportunity,
although a handful of individual schools did book in the
following year. How to sell extra weeks during the
summer holidays was also considered, including letting
to outside businesses and to social services for children
under their care. Clearly the centre was not going to
thrive unless it was booked for as many weeks as
possible during the year. 32 school groups stayed at the
OTC in 1982. Then in 1983 34 schools had groups stay

at the centre, of these 24 were from ILEA, while the others came from Berkshire (7), Hampshire (1),
Richmond on Thames (1) and Surrey (1). A continuing deficit caused ongoing concern.

The farm, however, was developing nicely. TVS donated a Land Rover,
and the tractor, donated by Ford, was extremely useful. A sow and litter
were donated by the Beaulieu Young Farmers Club, and a greenhouse
was erected in memory of Mr Clarke, brother of Miss Clarke, the bursar.
The children spent 50% of their time on the farm involved in farm
studies and practical farm work. Other activities included time out in

the New Forest and on the
coast, the Riverside Walk
and Buckler's Hard, a visit to
Salisbury Market, and even
pony riding. For London
children it was an incredible
experience, so completely
different from anything they
were able to do at home that
it made a lasting impression
on them.

In order to improve and enhance all the facilities, teaching
activities, and publicity of the centre, an application was made to
the Manpower Services Commission for two full-time and five
part time staff to assist with the work. This way the teaching was
expanded, the buildings and yard were repaired and improved,
and much work was done to make the farm more available and
understandable to the visitors.

Out of Town Centre 1984 - 86

By 1984 the farm stock had increased considerably. A group of cows, calves, heifers and steers amounting to 58 animals, plus a bull, made a sizeable herd. There were also 2 breeding sows with 30 young pigs, 2 nanny goats, and a considerable number of geese, ducks and laying hens.

The facilities at the centre were now much improved. However, a farm assistant was required, plus more equipment and an additional building for housing animals in winter were needed. A request was made for a tipping trailer, a muck spreader and hay turner, and materials to build a covered yard. The uptake of services remained lower than was needed to ensure that the income covered all the expenses and developments, so vigorous marketing was needed. If more residential weeks could be sold that would help the finances enormously, and at the same time, it would give opportunity for more children to benefit from the wonderful services on offer.

For the residential groups, teaching continued to be supported by a member of staff from the Countryside Education Trust for 2 days each week, although by February 1984 it was being provided on a voluntary basis.

In 1984 Jack Hargreaves retired as Chairman of the Out of Town Country Pursuits Centre. He would also cease to be involved with film making and wanted to retire from public life, so his involvement with the centre came to an end.

The year 1984/85 saw an increase in occupation to 40 booked weeks. This was acknowledged with great enthusiasm and increased finances considerably, much to everyone's relief.

More work was done on the farm to improve the buildings and the facilities available, and increase the equipment. The covered yard was built to house the cattle in the winter with the help of workers under the Manpower Services Project, and a cattle crush was bought to improve the handling of stock. An incubator was also provided and chicks started to be produced on a regular basis. The children loved to see them hatch and when they were allowed to hold them they were really delighted. The pigs and piglets were also a firm favourite, and as three sows produced a total of 21 piglets early in 1986 there was plenty to keep the children's interest.

The residential centre was running well. The staff were providing an excellent service to visiting groups, and the number of booked groups rose to 41 for the first time.

During 1986 the land at Moonhills Farm, of approximately 29 acres, became available and Charlie Knight suggested that the additional land would increase the efficiency of the farm. The land was drier and therefore easier to manage than many areas of the existing land, which could be seriously waterlogged in prolonged wet weather. The number of animals, particularly sheep, that could be kept would be substantially increased, which would give a better financial return. Dave Robinson was also enthusiastic and felt that it would increase the interest and educational opportunities for the children. Arrangements were therefore made with the estate for the OTC to lease this additional acreage.

A further application was made to the Manpower Services Commission for six workers to take part in the community project at the Out of Town Centre for the following year. It was an ambitious scheme and the proposed work included; practical tasks with small groups of children, the development of bee-keeping on the farm, assistance in organising off-site activities with the warden, production of a video and other educational materials, a monthly newsletter for schools, and building work on the farm. In addition, there was a small kitchen garden that had existed for some time, positioned on the left of the entrance where a car park and grass area was laid out later. This was to be further developed under the MSC Project with a greenhouse and improved beds

and paths, so they would certainly be kept busy. The application was successful, but it took some time to appoint the staff needed. Even so, building work went ahead to construct an extension to the barn. Not all the elements of the scheme were achieved that year but it was agreed that the MSC Project was proving extremely valuable to the centre.

The permanent staff on 1st July 1986 were as follows:
        David Robinson - Head of Centre
        Charlie and Elaine Knight - Farm Management
        Sue Elliot - Secretary
        Jenny Livermore - Housekeeper
        Vivien Trollope - Cook
        Angela Filmore - Assistant Cook
        Terry Gover - Farm Assistant
        Barbara Nielsen and Marion King - Domestic
                                Assistants

The fact that the staffing had remained stable for some time was proving to be a major contribution to the smooth running of the centre. The bookings remained high with 40 weeks booked and further groups expressing interest in making bookings. Mr Urquhart had completed a really good quality promotional video, which would be used in the ongoing fund raising, so everyone was very positive about the work.

OTC 1987

By 1987 the lease on the new land at Moonhills had been finalised and extra stock had been introduced. The drier land at Moonhills meant that both cattle and sheep could be kept outside there during the winter and the numbers increased. This meant more animals were available to sell, which added substantially to the farm income, as well as providing additional interest for the children.

A group from the Sanders Watney Driving Club for the Disabled booked for a week in the summer holidays, and there were some groups from Hampshire Social Services. This was an extra challenge to the staff, but a really important way for the centre to increase bookings and widen its services. A number of new sponsors and charitable trusts had gained an interest in the work of the Out of Town Centre at this time, so it was especially important that the centre was seen to be meeting the needs of as wide a range of people as possible. Fundraising, however, was still a very big issue at all Governors Meetings and it was proposed that a paid fundraiser should be employed. The Ernest Cook Foundation was approached to sponsor this post.

On the farm, the need was seen to replace the breeding ewes. It was proposed that ewe lambs of good quality and of a highly productive, commercially viable breed, should be purchased. To achieve this 20 lambs would be purchased each year from 1987 – 89, bringing the flock up to 60. This would generate a significant income and help to reduce the farm deficit, which had continued to be a concern each year.

By 1987 the programme was well established. The children loved feeding the animals each morning and evening, and the time they spent on the farm amounted to about half of the total time they were at the centre. Special activities such as cultivation, haymaking and sheep shearing were of particular interest, but the regular weekly programme of land use mapping, animal studies, field surveys, studies of hedgerows, buildings and machinery were also a great delight. Even mucking out the animals was approached with great glee by most young visitors. In the evenings they recorded their days' activities in a great variety of ways including; pictures and sketches, graphs and photographs, and tape and video recordings. Some schools even included acting and drama to enrich the experience for their children, and each evening one child was given the privilege of completing a page of the OTC diary.

Off-site activities continued to include visits to the Salisbury cattle market. This was particularly interesting if Out of Town Centre animals were being bought or sold, and the children took great interest in the prices paid. Park Farm on the Beaulieu Estate was also a popular destination where large scale commercial farming could be demonstrated. Other visits included were the Hampshire Farm Museum, outings into the New Forest itself, and visits to the Woodland Study Centre. Groups could also visit Buckler's Hard, study the development of the river and river estuary,

do coastal and beach studies at Lepe, and see the birds at Needs Ore from the specially constructed bird hide. There was even an opportunity to do horse riding or go to the Isle of Wight for the day. The programme was certainly very wide and varied, and visiting school staff often found it difficult to choose from all the exciting possibilities on offer.

The first Out of Town Centre Open Day was held on 20th September 1987. An arena was set up in the top field where there was a range of interesting displays from heavy horses to a motor bike display team, and all types of farming and countryside activities. Tractor rides took the visitors around the site and there were pony rides for the children. The pigeon shoot was a bit remote from the main activities so perhaps one of the less successful ventures, but the domestic staff produced a wonderful range of foods within the residential centre and there was a BBQ outside to complete the catering for visitors. Stalls and sideshows provided interest and contributed to the financial success of the day which did provide a modest profit. Naturally there were ways in which the event could be improved, but it was counted a great success and plans were put in place to repeat it in the following year.

In the autumn of 1987 there was a devastating storm that caused much damage on the farm. This included damage to the dutch barn, covered yard and the loose boxes. The slate roofs on the loose boxes were a particular problem as they had been in need of extensive repair before the storm and the insurance company was naturally reluctant to pay for any of the additional damage incurred. In the kitchen garden the greenhouse had been completely destroyed, so the storm clearly caused a number of problems, but it was agreed that many other places had suffered much more damage and the OTC was fortunate not to be more badly affected. During the following year agreement was reached with the insurance company and repairs

were completed to the buildings and the greenhouse was replaced.

The ILEA had been one of the two major sponsors of the Out of Town Centre from its inception in 1980. More than half the schools attending the centre had come from London and had been part of the block booking made by ILEA. However, in 1988 the government decided that ILEA should be abolished to take effect from 1st April 1990. This was a major crisis for the centre. Even with the support of ILEA the OTC had run at a deficit each year and only survived by strenuous fundraising efforts by both Governors and staff. Mr Date, the Company Secretary, had been appointed as fundraiser the previous year, which had proved to be a positive step. A further blow occurred when the MSC Scheme was discontinued and this valuable source of extra labour was withdrawn. This placed an enormous additional strain on OTC staff who had benefited from both practical and teaching support. It did, in fact, make it impossible for the summer teaching programme to be carried out without employing a teaching assistant and arrangements had to be made for the autumn term and the future.

Bookings within the residential centre were maintained in 1988 with 45 weeks booked. Marketing the centre was of vital importance, though, if booking levels were to be maintained in future years. Schools in London boroughs and in Berkshire and Hampshire were circulated with details of the Centre. Dave Robinson visited teachers' centres and promoted the work and facilities, and a lot of interest was generated.

The farm continued to develop with a good range of crops grown in rotation, which not only improved the land, but increased the educational potential enormously. The crops included winter wheat, winter and spring barley, kale, vegetables and fodder crops, lucerne and grass leys. The land at Moonhills was now fully integrated into the management of the farm, and an acre of land was set aside to grow strawberries there. It was hoped that this would provide a significant income for the farm over the next 5 years.

The rearing of beef cattle remained the farm's major enterprise as far as the animals were concerned. There were 15 suckler cows with their calves at this time, plus 16 weaned calves and 9 yearlings, so it was a significant herd. A small number of dairy cows was also kept, which included one Jersey cow that was hand milked, and two Guernsey and one Shorthorn used as nurse cows for 3 Friesian calves. The sheep flock consisted of 47 ewes and a good quality Suffolk ram. It was hoped that about 70 lambs would be born in March 1989 and the flock would be increased further.

The other stock on the farm, although secondary in importance to the cattle and sheep in economic terms, provided a very important contribution to the educational experience of the children. There were two breeding sows and a landrace boar, and a litter of 9 saddleback piglets from which two gilts were to be retained for future breeding. These were kept in the pigsties that faced down onto the farm from the Victorian building, later converted to a classroom. A wide variety of poultry was kept so that the centre was self-sufficient in eggs, and an incubation programme was run within the Centre so the children could see the baby chicks hatch out. This always caused great excitement and delight.

Out of Town Centre 1988 -91

1988 was a difficult year. On one hand the farm and centre were providing first class educational and residential opportunities for over 1300 school children, while in the background the very life of the centre was threatened by changes in policy at Government level. Many ILEA field studies centres were being closed and the changes to the MSC scheme were going to have devastating effects on all those who were relying on staff provided under the programme. In contrast to the problems the end of year accounts for April 1988 showed a surplus for the first time, thanks to the hard work of many in raising funds and donations. Many urgent meetings were arranged for the Governors to try to resolve the problems.

Work continued on repairs to the looseboxes, the new greenhouse was erected, work to repair the barn was put in hand. The MSC extended the existing scheme until 29th July which gave a welcome breathing space, so the work at the Centre continued.

ILEA cancelled 5 weeks of bookings but most of these were re-let to other schools. On the farm the weather caused problems. A very wet spring followed by a very dry early summer affected crop development, and badly hit the new pick your own strawberry project. Although the silage was successfully harvested, the hay was delayed. The cattle were unaffected and a good price was received for fat cattle sold in early summer, and many good quality lambs were born. A new tractor was promised by Ford of Britain and was delivered before the end of the year.

There were some staff changes too. Mrs Elliott who had served the Centre well for many years, resigned as secretary and Mrs Livermore was appointed to replace her. This moved her from the position of housekeeper. Dave Robinson was being put under increasing strain towards the end of the year and, as no additional help was found for the teaching programme, he was having to manage entirely by himself.

The Open Day, held in October, was a lovely event and it made a profit of over £2000. However, it took a great deal of work to organise and required a great deal of input from the staff, so careful thought had to be given as to whether it would become an annual event. Certainly many volunteers and local people supported and helped with it so it was good for public relations and gave more people a feeling of involvement in the work of the Centre.

A further blow at the end of the year was another Government policy change. The DES (Department of Education and Science) put forward new guidelines for schools organising visits to residential centres. These were quite difficult to understand and many schools were uncertain how it would affect them. This led to late cancellations of existing bookings and a reluctance on the part of schools to make future bookings. It was well into 1989 before schools began to understand the new rules and found ways to work with them.

In 1989 a 'League of Friends' organisation was set up. It had three main aims: a) to improve relations with the local community and others associated with the Centre, b) to engage in activities which support the Centre and enhance the provision available to visiting children, and c) to seek to raise funds for the Centre. This was well supported by a number of local people who gave support in many different ways.

By the end of 1989 ILEA had been abolished and this made the Out of Town Centre much more independent of outside influences, but at the same time it caused considerable financial problems and schools were unsure about the future of the centre. The earlier close working relationship with the Countryside Education Trust had become more and more distant during the 1980s as the farm and residential facilities were developed at Home Farm, and the day services and community programme progressed in Hartford Wood. However, in the new educational climate it was felt that it would be of benefit to both organisations to renew their relationship and work more closely together. There could be more joint projects and greater use of each other's services. The teaching staff at the Woodland Study Centre could support the educational programme at the residential centre and give wider opportunities for the children. Schools that had used the residential services before were contacted and made aware that the Centre was continuing to provide the high level of service they had experienced in the past and that new opportunities were becoming available. It was hoped that they would be encouraged to make further bookings.

It was decided that the Open Day was something that had contributed a great deal to the life of the Out of Town Centre, not so much in financial terms but in bringing the community together, so another one was planned for September 1989. There were marquees with items for sale by the WI and other local organisations. There was an arena with all sorts of demonstrations from tractors and dogs to a motor cycle display team and a fairground with swingboats and roundabout to attract the children. The local ferret club kept everyone amused with ferret races, and there were a variety of demonstrations and sideshows. There were a number of fundraising stalls including bowling for the pig and all the usual attractions of the farm animals were there to be enjoyed. The local Beaulieu fire service turned out with a fire engine and local contractor, Bill Niccolls, provided a

crane with an aerial runway to add to the excitement. A splendid agricultural band called 'The Plonkers' provided a musical backdrop and the atmosphere of the whole event was superb. Once again it made a profit of about £2,000, but its attraction in the local community far outweighed the size of the monetary income.

Despite every effort on behalf of staff, Governors and Friends, 1990 was a disappointing year. Residential bookings were reduced and income did not come up to expectations or needs. The autumn Open Day was an even greater success financially with an income of £4,000, but even this could not allay the anxiety that the Centre was getting deeper and deeper in debt.

On 1st April 1991 ILEA came to an end and before long the Governors of the Centre were told that the accumulated debt was such that, under company law, they were obliged to cease trading.

Abbotswood Junior School
Ringwood Road
Totton
Hampshire
SO40 8EB

8th June 2005

Dear Anna and Linda,
         I am writing to thank you for a brilliant day at Beaulieu Study
Center yesterday. My favourite part of the day the minibeasts because everybody found
some & very interesting ones. I learnt that worms have a very strange way of moving.
The part of the day that I found most interesting was doing the pond dipping because
of all the different creatures that everybody found there.
Thank you again for a super day.
                        Yours Sincerely,
                        Daniel Buckingham

Chapter 3

Countryside Education Trust 1976 - 1978

From the Autumn of 1976 the Countryside Education Trust and the Out of Town Centre were two separate organisations. Graham continued to be involved in the Out of Town Centre, but his main focus was the development of educational services for the Motor Museum, Palace House and Beaulieu Abbey, Buckler's Hard, and for the wider Estate. This all had to be financed by funds raised from anywhere they could be obtained, and it was not proving to be very easy.

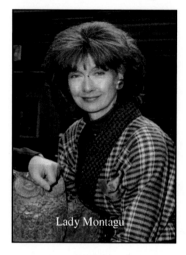
Lady Montagu

Lady Montagu had already shown a keen interest in helping raise funds for the CET and by March 1977 she had got together a group of enthusiastic volunteers to form a Fundraising Committee. This group would produce a programme of events for the year, and hoped to contribute worthwhile sums of money to help the work to go forward. One of the first events planned was a Christmas Fair in Palace House at the beginning of December. In addition, people were to be encouraged to become Friends of the Trust and volunteer to help with the great range of projects that were being carried out. By the middle of 1977 there were 83 Friends of the Trust.

A set of slides was put together to promote the work. They could be made available to Trustees, staff and volunteers so they could give talks and slide presentations to anyone interested, and especially those who might sponsor the work.

Plans for a major Countryside Centre at Keeping Copse, between Buckler's Hard and Bailey's Hard, were in hand. The Centre would comprise a small interpretive building, a series of thematic trails and wayside displays that would fit in with, and compliment, the educational interpretation of Buckler's Hard. The vacated amusement hut within the Beaulieu Complex, which was being used by school groups visiting the Motor Museum and Palace House and Abbey, could be moved to the site in the autumn. However, before these plans could be put into operation, it was found that the brickworks at Bailey's Hard would be becoming vacant and there may be a possibility of developing that as a countryside and riverside centre.

Meanwhile, there was considerable pressure on Graham's time. While still trying to establish a centre for the CET he was often drawn away by his work for the Country House Estate and for Education Projects for the Heritage Education Year. Over 50 Historic Houses had requested visits. All this extra work meant that more secretarial help was needed to enable him to fulfil these commitments. He was able to obtain a grant of £1,000 to fund this, but it was still putting a strain on Trust's funds and staff and diverting Graham from the task of developing the educational services on the Beaulieu Estate.

The governments scheme to help the unemployed was continuing, and a new MSC team of three teachers, a designer and a general assistant were appointed to carry on the work started by the team appointed the previous year. These new staff soon got to work producing new resource materials, including film strips and slide shows on the New Forest and Beaulieu Estate, and study packs on Salisbury, Christchurch, the Isle of Wight and other local sites. It was intended that these should be used by students on day visits or staying at the Out of Town Centre. They also organised a very successful fortnight of Holiday Activities during the summer of 1977. They were for children aged 9 - 13 and included a forest walk, map reading, forest crafts, survival, and local and natural history. They were so popular and over-subscribed that it was planned to provide more holiday activities the following year.

Countryside Education Stands Alone

By the middle of 1978 it was clear that careful thought needed to be given to the organisation of the Countryside Education Trust. The services within the Museum complex and Buckler's Hard had become very successful, and the wider work all over the estate was flourishing, but funding the work had become really difficult, and Graham needed to spend more time at Beaulieu for the work to be developed further. So it was decided that Graham would discontinue his advisory work, and he and his Assistant should leave the staff of the CET and be employed in future by Montagu Ventures Ltd. MVL would be responsible for Education at Beaulieu, which would include all the museums services. Then 25% of Graham's and his administrator's time would be given to

the CET free of charge in order that they could run the countryside and environmental education throughout the wider estate. This change soon benefitted the CET as the financial worry was removed and there was more scope for development. The CET and Education at Beaulieu continued to work very closely together and were awarded the prestigious Sandford Award that year for services to education, which was presented at the Tower of London the following year.

Graham did much work to ensure that Local Education Authorities and teachers not only heard about the CET, but became involved in planning the services on offer. There was a real demand from local LEAs for more curriculum-orientated environmental services for secondary schools, while more distant urban LEAs wanted more general services. Further Teachers' Open Days were advertised and well attended.

Changes were taking place within the Manpower Services Commission at this time. In future there would be a section specifically to encourage young people called Y.O.P. (Youth Opportunities Programme), and another called S.T.E.P. (first step into work for graduates) that would provide opportunities for the adult unemployed. For the Trust there would be one person employed under the Y.O.P. scheme and eight under the S.T.E.P. scheme. There would be three teachers, two designers, one secretary, one joiner and one archive assistant.

Although there had been much discussion about a centre based at the Brickworks at Bailey's Hard it was proving very difficult to raise sufficient finance to convert the buildings and realise this opportunity. Funds were also being sought to restore and develop Beaulieu Mill so it

would take some time before either of these buildings would be available for Trust use. It was, however, becoming essential to provide a base outside the tourist areas so that secondary school field studies might be pursued. It was felt that the Hut that had been used so successfully at the Motor Museum would be adequate for the time being, and it was suggested that this should be sited in Hartford Wood. The position would be close to the road so services could be put in, and parking could be in the main car parks at the Motor Museum. A planning application had to be made, and then arrangements made to level the site, move the building and make toilet arrangements, but all this could be achieved at very modest cost with the help of the S.T.E.P. team.

By the middle of 1979 plans were well advanced for the establishment of the Out of Town Centre. The building work was progressing well and the official opening was planned for 25th April 1980. A Warden and Farmer had been appointed and the Executive Secretary would also be in place in September. So 1980 was a real landmark for the Countryside Education Trust. The original idea to promote education on the Beaulieu Estate had now developed into three separately funded organisations; The Countryside Education Trust, Education at Beaulieu and the Out of Town Centre. These three would provide a vibrant, exciting, comprehensive and inclusive educational service that would make every part of the Beaulieu Estate available for visitors to experience and enjoy. They continued to work closely together sharing expertise, equipment, office accommodation and staff and the original Director, Graham Carter, continued to be involved in each one.

Education Staff Appointed

Kate Glegg

On 1st June 1980 a Countryside Education Officer, Kate Glegg, was appointed to the staff of the Countryside Education Trust. This position was supported by grants from ILEA and Hampshire County Council. Her work would include two days teaching of students staying at the Out of Town Centre and three days working for the CET. She was well qualified for the post with degrees in Geography and Biology, and teaching experience up to 6th form at secondary school. She had also carried out research on vegetation in the New Forest, and was organising the Conservation Corps for Somerset. She would be very capable of delivering the teaching programme and organising staff and volunteers

Graham had arranged for several of the local farms to be used as venues for the farm teaching programme. These included Park Farm on the Beaulieu Estate and Thorns Farm at Sowley. Farm visits were very popular with school groups and other farms on the Cadland and Exbury Estates were suggested as appropriate venues. Both Maldwin and Gilly Drummond were closely involved with the CET at this time, and keen to welcome visitors to the Cadland Estate.

The Out of Town residential centre was operating well and progress was being made on the construction of new loose boxes and other buildings at the farm. Bookings from ILEA and other authorities were excellent, although the response from Hampshire had been disappointing. With so many groups using the residential facilities there was much need of the teaching resources of the CET which had been provided by a former member of the STEP team until Kate was in post and able to take over. This she did with great enthusiasm and expertise.

In 1980 the CET ran 3 weeks of holiday activities for children aged 8 - 13 years. The very exciting and ambitious programme was as follows:

Holiday Activities

Monday	Beaulieu scavenger hunt, Woodland Nature Trail, Art and Crafts (kite making, clay modelling, T-shirt printing, etc)
Tuesday	Understanding maps and a cross country hike. Swimming.
Wednesday	Assault course at Marchwood Army Camp and a trip to the Fawley Power Station Marine Research Laboratory. Photography (Veteran car). Games and swimming
Thursday	Printing photographs and a Need's Ore visit.
Friday	Survival techniques in the wild. It's a knock-out. Barbeque (6.00 - 8.00 pm)

There was also a training course for 30 volunteers starting in September 1980 that lasted the whole year.
The programme was as follows:

<u>The Volunteer Training Course</u>
Autumn Term
1.	Introductory Woodland Walk and an introduction to the work of the Countryside Education Trust.
2.	Introduction to the resources of the Beaulieu Estate and area:
   (i)	The Beaulieu River and National Nature Reserve
   (ii)	Hartford Wood and forestry
   (iii)	Farming and the Out of Town Centre project
   (iv)	The New Forest and Beaulieu
3.	Introduction to the environment
   (i)	Environmental education
   (ii)	Basic concepts of ecology
   (iii)	Man and the environment

Spring Term
	A series of specific habitat studies and visits to other
countryside establishments

Summer Term
1.	Introduction to field work and to techniques used in various habitat studies
2.	Communication techniques in environmental education
3.	Opportunity for project work and an optional examination

The Holiday Activities and the Volunteer Training Course were very well received. There was also a residential course for History undergraduates. Hartford Wood and the Riverside Walk between Beaulieu and Buckler's Hard were being well used, and there were several group visits to Need's Ore. The education provided by the CET had certainly made great progress in scope and depth.

The Woodland Study Centre and Manpower Services Commission

By September 1980 plans were well advanced for moving the Hut from the Motor Museum site to Hartford Wood. A group from the Youth Opportunities Programme (YOP) had been working on the estate from June that year and had already spent time on clearing and renovating the Beehive Brick Kiln at Bailey's Hard. This had been so successful that there had been discussions with Michelmersh Brick Co Ltd as to the best procedure for a celebratory firing of the kiln. So a good team was

already in place to start laying the foundations and moving the Hut to Hartford Wood and Graham had raised the funds to make this possible. The work went ahead and, by April 1981, Kate was able to report to the Trustees that the basic structure had been erected. The Hut was to be known as the Woodland Study Centre and, after services had been connected, and basic toilet facilities had been

provided, it came into use in July. There was still much work to be done on the inside fittings, shelving and storage space but these continued throughout the summer and autumn, producing a building that had been constructed and finished to a high standard throughout.

Another exciting facility made available to the CET was a workboat called 'Hippo' that was provided and equipped by the Nature Conservancy Council (NCC). James Venner was the Warden of the Nature Reserve at Needs Ore, and with his help, the boat could be made available to 'O' and 'A' level students for Marine Studies. There could be 10 students per trip and they would run from Buckler's Hard down river to Need's Ore and around Gull Island. This would be linked to shore based marine work, or a complete survey of the river, combined with the Riverside Walk.

Study books, trails and guided walks were produced to guide and educate visitors, and a big publicity drive was planned to inform schools and colleges about all the new and exciting facilities available through the CET.

Staffing at this time consisted of Graham Carter - Director, Kate Glegg - Countryside Education Officer, a team from the Youth Opportunity Programme led by their supervisor John Scott Robinson, and three people appointed under the MSC Community Enterprise Programme: Terry Williams - teacher, Nick Hatchley - artist designer, and Sam Simms - carpenter. These were assisted by volunteers and members of estate staff. Two who were particularly appreciated for their contributions were Peter Murfin and James Venner. Others mentioned by name were Paul Goodson, Caroline Pike, Ann C, Hilary Booth,

Sue Roper and Di Smith. The Out of Town Centre education programme was assisted on two days each week by CET staff, which was a major commitment from such a small team of people.

In 1983 the MSC Community Programme had been so successful that Graham asked that the team be increased to 14 people plus a supervisor. Some of these were full-time and some part-time, but they included teachers, research officers, a forester, a designer, a clerical worker, builders, carpenters and manual workers. These were paid for by the government scheme and were given valuable experience that enabled them to move on to full employment when they left the CET. This continued in 1984/85 with 2 supervisors and 21 workers.

With all these staff available, well motivated and supervised, an enormous amount of work could be achieved. The Woodland Study Centre was well decorated within and without with fascinating and highly artistic displays and exhibitions. Stuffed animals were introduced to enliven the teaching programme, particularly for younger children, so they would have the experience of seeing and touching real wild animals. How spikey is a hedgehog and how rough is the coat of a badger? What do feathers feel like? Are

they soft or hard? Do all birds feel the same? These questions and many others could be answered, also the relationship between different animals, the food chain and the web of life could be demonstrated. Outside live animals and birds were kept. A pair of Barn Owls and a Little Owl, a male ferret, a warren full of rabbits and a pair of Mallard Ducks were all cared for by the team and introduced to the young visitors.

Other projects were in hand around Hartford Wood. A trail that started out on the Forest near Hilltop traced the Hartford Stream down through the wood. On its way the source of the stream could be investigated, followed by a series of fish tanks that had been used in the past as a fish farm. These were renovated, cleared and provided with new sluices. Next came Top Pond suffering from encroachment from surrounding

vegetation. That would be a project deferred to a later date. Middle Pond, lower down the valley, was to provide regular pond dipping experiences and fresh water ecological studies for visitors, so that needed to be tackled more quickly. It had to be cleared of vegetation, the dam retaining it had to be reinforced and a new weir constructed. When all that was completed, platforms and walkways had to be built to allow access. This was a very big project, but not beyond the capabilities of the team.

Coppicing and a Bird Hide at Needs Ore

It was in 1983 that an area of woodland near the Centre was compartmentalised to form a seven year rotation plot for coppicing. Each year one section would be cut to the ground so that it would re-grow primarily to provide materials for hurdle making, although other products would be harvested in later years. This would allow an increase in diversity of habitats with ground flora flourishing again as it had in the past when the wood was coppiced regularly. Lessons in woodland management could be included in the curriculum and there would be a big increase in butterflies and other insects that could be observed and monitored.

A meadow was also fenced off at the bottom of the wood that would be managed in a way that would encourage the growth of wild flowers and grasses suitable for butterflies and moths. A selection of basket willows was planted in one corner, and it was hoped that this would provide materials in a year or two for other interesting activities. It was a lot of

work, however, to keep it weeded so that it would have a chance to establish and grow strongly.

There were so many exciting and interesting courses for adults and visiting school groups to attend that it is difficult to describe them all, but they included an enormous range, from arts and crafts to ecological studies, and from the work of the countryside to country crafts. Well known professional people were happy to be involved, with Simon King, Johnny Morris and Sir Peter Scott all giving talks. Over 2,500 children were taught in organised groups, Holiday activities were well attended at Easter, Summer and in the Autumn, and an Edwardian Christmas programme in Palace House was enthusiastically received. In all, over 4,250 people used the services of the CET in 1983.

While all the developments were going on in the surrounds of the Woodland Study Centre and Hartford Wood, much work was progressing elsewhere. At Need's Ore Nature Reserve a bird hide was built and access paths established with screens provided to shield visitors as they approached the hide. A new display

was created that would be used at the Buckler's Hard Village Festival, and a screen printing workshop set up in the Mill Building in Beaulieu. Other organisations were also developing in the area. Richard Lynnes was setting up an organisation called Beaulieu Pursuits

which provided a ropes course in a small part of Hartford Wood north of Hides Close. Co-operation with the CET was quickly established. The expertise of staff at the CET was also recognised by a group establishing a Nature Reserve at Forest Front in Dibden Purlieu and they were asked to be involved in an advisory capacity.

In 1984 the second coppice coup was cut. The first one was growing on nicely and the range of flowers appearing was wonderful to see. A woodland charcoal camp was set up with the help of Jack Langley, a local charcoal maker, to demonstrate the traditional method of making charcoal in an earth clamp. Some demonstration clamps were set up to show how it was built, and a final one for burning. A hydraulic ram had been discovered in the wood, and this was renovated by Green and Carter Ltd and set up just below Middle Pond to pump water to a pond that had been constructed outside the Woodland Study Centre. It was fascinating to see how the ram could pump water for nearly half a mile just using the water pressure of the stream flowing into it.

A chalet was donated to the CET by the Master Builder's House Hotel. It was situated at Buckler's Hard and refurbished to make an ideal base for Riverside and Nature Reserve work, and studies of Buckler's Hard itself. The brick kiln at Bailey's Hard was re-pointed and in the best condition it had been for many years. All those using the Riverside Walk were able to see it, and could better understand how bricks were fired. A Riverside Walk leaflet had been produced to explain all the features along the route.

An Education Officer and a Community Officer

Finances by 1983/84 were looking much healthier than they had in the early years. Graham, with help from his secretary, Ann Matthews, had obtained a range of grants from Local Authorities, Charitable Trusts and industry; special grants for specific projects had been given. Lady Montagu and the Fundraising Committee had done a wonderful job of raising funds through events and the Christmas Fair, and other Trustees and friends had either raised funds or recommended possible sponsors. Government funds for the Manpower Services Commission Community Project was of immense importance in providing staff, equipment and running costs, and the Trust was proving very successful in every aspect of its work.

When Esso agreed to sponsor the work of the CET's community programme, a Project Officer, David Fisher, was appointed to the Trust to start work on 7th January 1985. He was very

David Quoroll

experienced, and had run a number of in-house training days for teachers in London and soon got to work developing an interesting and inspiring range of activities suitable for all ages. Staffing, however, was not without its problems as Kate tendered her resignation to take effect from 21st December 1984. She was moving to Scotland to get married, and it was agreed that a replacement for her would be urgently needed. Graham had been seeking funding from Hampshire Education Authority to help finance this post and in April he was able to confirm that a levy of £8,500 had been granted. Consequently the post of Countryside Education Officer was advertised and in due course David Quoroll was appointed to start at the end of July 1985. He was 28 years old, a Biology graduate, and a qualified teacher, who had spent the last 5 years teaching at the Field Studies Council's Draper Centre in Wales. Terry Williams who had been supervisor of the MSC Team for 3 years was retained to bridge the gap between Kate leaving and David starting.

Also in 1985 the Government changed the criteria for those eligible to take part in the MSC Team. This made it more difficult to recruit suitable people to fill the posts and consequently there was a reduction in services and developments, much to the disappointment of everybody.

David Fisher was very active during the year, and when he gave his report after only 6 months in the post it was astounding how much he had achieved. He had visited 13 different schools during the period, and had helped four of them set up environmental areas with ponds, at their own premises. He had made contact with a dozen other organisations including Mid-Hants Teacher's Centre, the BTCV, Hampshire Garden's Trust, The County Planning Department and the Waterside Council for Community Services. He had done many days of teaching and was running three clubs for children and young people - Saturday Club, Senior Conservation Group and Beaulieu Young Ornithology Club (YOC). In addition, he had prepared a programme of courses and lectures for the months ahead, arranged further visits to schools and other organisations, and represented the Trust, (and his sponsors, Esso) at shows and country Fairs.

In November that year Graham reported that Hampshire C C had agreed to give a grant of £8,000 in return for all Hampshire schools visiting the Woodland Study Centre free of charge, this was in addition to the money to support the post of Education Officer. There was still a very limited number of centres offering field studies and environmental education so the services of the CET were much valued.

In order to advertise Education at Beaulieu, which included all the services at the Motor Museum, Palace House, Buckler's Hard and everything offered by the CET, a new leaflet was produced. This was in full colour for the first time, and was circulated to all schools, pre-schools and colleges within reasonable travelling distance of Beaulieu. In addition to this, a newsletter was sent out to all Hampshire schools giving details of new courses that were being offered for the autumn and winter months. These included how

plants and animals survive the winter by hibernation, adaptation or migration. Until then the great majority of visitors had only come in the summer. There was also an Open Day in October to which all primary and middle school teachers were invited. Many came with their families and thoroughly enjoyed the day. For pre-school groups, David Fisher organised an Open Day in September which was well attended and soon resulted in more than 250 student bookings for that age group.

Meanwhile David Quoroll was investigating the possibility of encouraging secondary schools to use CET services. There had been a change to the examination structure which was to replace 'O' level GCE and CSE exams with GCSEs. These included a much greater environmental content and many teachers felt ill equipped to teach ecology and so four new courses were prepared to meet this need. They were: Air Pollution and Acid Rain; Feeding Structure of a Freshwater System; Soils, Environment and Plant Growth; and Populations - Changes and Control. Enquiries from colleges offering A-level studies were being carefully considered and new courses were prepared for those as well.

Great Success Then Dark Days

In 1986 the MSC team was again very successful. The scheme supervisor Koya Sylvest was able to move on to a permanent job and her position was taken by Michael Boase, who prove to be equally good. The enthusiasm and expertise of Keith Goodwin in Design, and Mark Hillyer in interpretation also added immeasurably to the success of the team.

During the year a caravan was donated to the Trust and positioned discreetely behind the Woodland Study Centre building. This was a big help in providing sufficient work space for all members of staff who needed to be on site. Until that time there was only the office for the staff to use, a room no more than 12ft x 10ft (10.8m x 9m), where all administrative work and preparation for teaching had to be done. Design staff members were able to use the flat over the garage associated with a terrace of cottages on the Motor Museum site. Hot air fan heaters were introduced in the WSC classroom because of the increased use in the colder months of the year, and hot water was available for the first time in the WSC storeroom, toilets and caravan. The toilet facilities, however, were very basic, consisting of two chemical toilets partitioned inside a garden shed. As visitor numbers increased this was proving to be less and less satisfactory and some larger adults found the cubicles too small. There was one memorable occasion when a very large teenage boy had to be sent out into the woodland when he just couldn't get into the toilets.

The publicity in the previous year had been so successful that the Woodland Study Centre was booked to capacity for 10 months of the year. This led to some concern as much of the teaching work was done by people on the MSC scheme, which was designed to enable people to get into full-time employment. The two main teachers under the scheme, Mark Hillyer and James Blake, were very good and really appreciated by visiting schools so it was quite possible that they would be offered teaching jobs before long. If that happened the CET could find itself with schools booked in and no one to teach them. A list of possible teachers to take groups in case of emergency had to be drawn up.

Holiday activities had become so popular that many children had to be turned away, and the bookings came in so quickly that it was difficult to keep pace with the demand. There were very few alternative opportunities in the area at that time, and Friends of the Trust or those who lived in the surrounding area were very upset if they failed to get a place. Five full weeks of activities were offered for younger children and they were booked up in a matter of days. For teenagers there was a really challenging programme of activities. There was a long distance cycle ride of 150 miles over 5 days, which followed the Esso Midline oil pipe line, and there was also a Solent Way Walk of 61 miles from Emsworth to Hurst Point. These were very popular with the more adventurous youngsters who didn't get many opportunities for this type of challenge.

The CET wanted to make more use of the Needs Ore Nature Reserve as much work had been done to provide hides and access paths. The boat, Hippo, was also being under used and James Venner was keen to help promote this. The biggest problem was lack of toilet facilities or undercover space if the weather proved inclement. Safety on Hippo was also an issue, so the CET and Richard Lynnes bought life jackets to share between the two organisations.

In 1987 the CET received its first minibus. It was a 17-seat bus and cost £800. This was a really large sum for the CET at that time and only made possible by a donation from TVS and funds raised by the Fundraising Committee. A payment of £1,000 per year was promised from Marks and Spencer for running costs. It was used for adult courses, A-level students using different parts of the Beaulieu estate, Holiday Activities and Saturday Clubs, which had now increased to four per month with the introduction of a WATCH Club.

The autumn of 1987 saw severe gales that affected the whole country and caused considerable damage in Hartford Wood. Some trees were blown down and others were left with limbs hanging dangerously. It needed a lot of work before it could be considered a safe place for groups to visit again. A great deal of this was done by the Beaulieu Estate staff.

It was with great sadness that Graham received the resignation of David Quoroll with effect from November 1987. This was followed by the news that the CET would not receive another MSC team when the existing team finished in February. Then David Fisher gave notice that he would be leaving in mid-February, coinciding with the termination of the MSC scheme. They were very dark days for the CET. Loss of the MSC team would reduce CET staff to a mere skeleton and services would have to be reduced accordingly. Esso confirmed that they would continue to support the Community post, and Hampshire Education Authority were approached to seek additional funding to support the educational work. Strenuous efforts were made to find other sponsors, but it was decided that temporary appointments of 2 teachers and one secretary/administrator be made for 6 months until more permanent funding could be obtained. Mike and Louise Shrubsole, who had been part of the final MSC team, were invited to stay on as the two teachers, and Rosalyn Reed was appointed as part-time

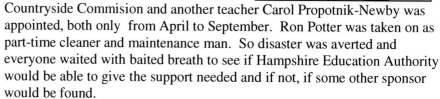

secretary/administrator until September. A second year student from Merrist Wood Agricultural College, Emma Slingsby, was accepted for a work placement partly supported by the Countryside Commision and another teacher Carol Propotnik-Newby was appointed, both only from April to September. Ron Potter was taken on as part-time cleaner and maintenance man. So disaster was averted and everyone waited with baited breath to see if Hampshire Education Authority would be able to give the support needed and if not, if some other sponsor would be found.

It was a very challenging summer term as bookings remained high and all staff had to work very hard to maintain the high standard of services for which the CET had become known. One notable feature was the Summer Holiday Activity programme which was called 'Monking About'. This was organised on a historical theme with Sue Tomkins, the Heritage Education Officer and Archivist for Montagu Ventures Ltd. Each of the 45 children taking part each week was provided with a monk's outfit, made by the CET staff. Activities included tile making, calligraphy and the history of the Cistercian monks in the cloisters of Beaulieu Abbey, a walk to see the Abbey Spring that supplied the monk's water supply, and a host of other craft activities and games around the Woodland Study Centre and Hartford Wood. It was a very ambitious programme and provided much fun for all concerned.

Countryside Education Trust 1988 - 90

By September Hampshire Education Authority had confirmed that they would give a grant of £36,000 per year to support teaching posts and administration, and Esso would continue to support the community programme. Mike Shrubsole was appointed Senior Education Officer with Philip Blandford and Carol Propotnik-Newby as Education Officers, (although Carol had to resign quite soon after and was replaced by Susan Anders). Vivien Drake became the Countryside and Community Officer and Rosalyn Reed was asked to stay on as part-time Administrator. With Ron Potter continuing as cleaner and maintenance man, the team was complete.

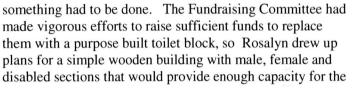

The condition of the toilet facilities at the Woodland Study Centre had become a real embarrassment and something had to be done. The Fundraising Committee had made vigorous efforts to raise sufficient funds to replace them with a purpose built toilet block, so Rosalyn drew up plans for a simple wooden building with male, female and disabled sections that would provide enough capacity for the number of visitors using the centre each day. This was submitted to the Planning Department of New Forest District Council and approved, and after suitable quotes had been obtained, the building was completed in time for the increase in visitors during the summer term of 1989. It was an enormous relief to have proper flushing toilets and hand washing facilities at last.

Viv Drake quickly got to work to provide a community programme for the year 1988/89. They included a Vegetarian Taste of Christmas, an illustrated talk by local wildlife photographers, boat trips, botanical illustration and a variety of other courses and lectures, all advertised in FACET. The Summer Holiday Activities for younger children were based at Buckler's Hard in 1989 under the title of 'Hearts of Oak and Jolly Tars' which proved to be great fun. For teenagers there was a mini-cycling break and a backpacking holiday. The Holiday Activities continued to be very popular and oversubscribed.

A Local Village Schools Initiative took place in spring 1989 with 250 pupils from local schools attending two mediaeval days. The first day provided 20 different mediaeval craft workshops run by Motor Museum staff, CET staff, Trustees and volunteers. Some were in the cloisters of Beaulieu Abbey, and others were at the Woodland Study Centre, and each child was able to move around trying several different ones during the day. The second day was a Country Fair when everyone came dressed in Mediaeval costume. Stalls were set up on part of the Motor Museum site with all sorts of medieval items that the children had made. The 'Lord of the Manor' and his wife arrived on horseback with great pageantry, and there were games and activities that would have been seen on a medieval market day. Everyone had a wonderful time and they were days that nobody involved would ever forget.

Teachers courses and open evenings continued to be well attended with 70 teachers taking part in one evening event. Schools very much appreciated the expertise of CET staff, and were keen to learn about how to present ecology and all environmental studies in practical ways. Graham, Mike and Philip were particularly knowledgeable. The teachers also wanted to know what was available to them for classes of all ages. The courses for younger children were delightful. To illustrate the programme for senses and adaptations there were specially made mole masks that the children wore as they felt their way along a rope trail, there was a squirrel branch laid along the ground for them to balance along, and a rabbit tunnel to crawl down chased by the wicked weasel! For the slightly older children there was pond dipping in the Middle Pond, now equipped with pond dipping platforms, and a enormous range of games and activities that would show them such things as how a tree worked, how a bat located its prey, what minibeasts lived on the woodland floor, and a host of others.

There was much contact with other local and national organisations and Viv was really beginning to make a name for herself in the area for her innovative and exciting events. She was able to arrange courses and lectures by people who have subsequently become very well known. Two of those involved were Ray Mears who led bushcraft courses, and Chris Packham who gave an interesting lecture on the New Forest. Local and national TV and other media began to take a real interest in what was going on at the CET.

Changes in staff were inevitable. In 1989 Susan Anders moved on to other things and Alison Staples became the new Education Officer.

The demand for CET services was such that a second centre along the Beaulieu River was still planned in order to increase capacity and scope. The Brickworks at Bailey's Hard had become available and Ralph Montagu agreed that it could become the Riverside Centre if sufficient funds could be raised. Change of use permission from the planning authority was granted in 1989, and in 1990 funds really started to come in. Hampshire County Council promised to support the project, National Power was interested in providing sponsorship, Southern Water would install toilet facilities, and it all looked very positive and exciting. However, it was not to be. The Beaulieu Estate needed to charge a lease for the building that would be unsustainable in the longer term and the project had to be abandoned.

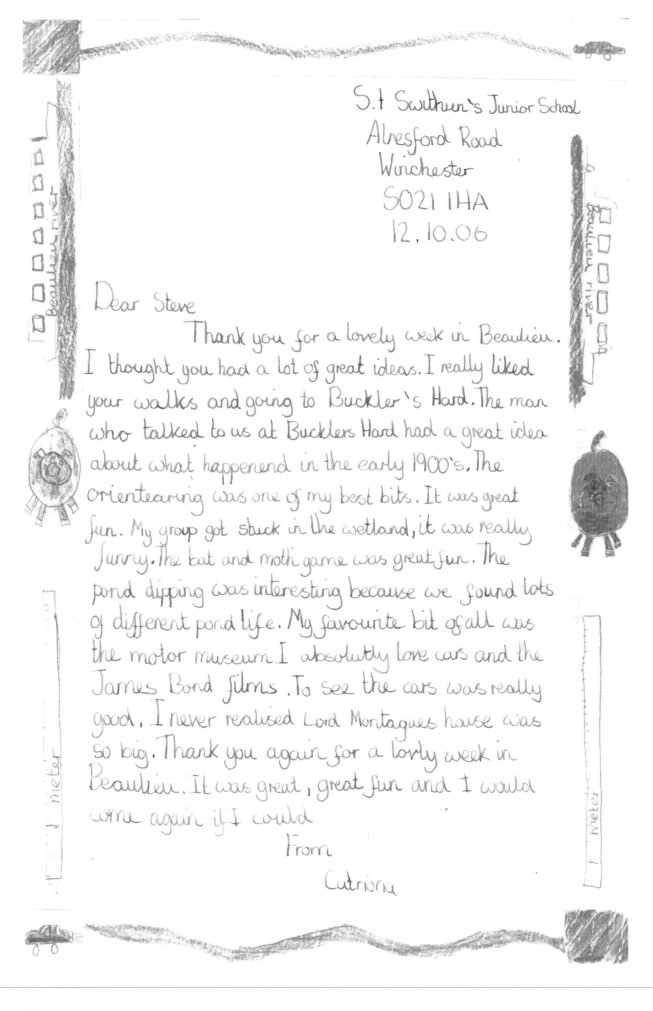

St Swithun's Junior School
Alresford Road
Winchester
SO21 1HA
12.10.06

Dear Steve
            Thank you for a lovely week in Beaulieu.
I thought you had a lot of great ideas. I really liked
your walks and going to Buckler's Hard. The man
who talked to us at Bucklers Hard had a great idea
about what happened in the early 1900's. The
orientearing was one of my best bits. It was great
fun. My group got stuck in the wetland, it was really
funny. The bat and moth game was great fun. The
pond dipping was interesting because we found lots
of different pond life. My favourite bit of all was
the motor museum I absolutly love cars and the
James Bond films. To see the cars was really
good. I never realised Lord Montagues house was
so big. Thank you again for a lovly week in
Beaulieu. It was great, great fun and I would
come again if I could
                          From

                          Catriona

Chapter 4

Countryside Education Trust & Out of Town Centre
1990 - 1991

On the 1st April 1990 the Inner London Education Authority (ILEA) was abolished. This had a devastating effect on the finances of the Out of Town Centre and put its very existence in jeopardy. From its foundation in 1978 the OTC had received a payment from ILEA amounting to the cost of 26 weeks residential courses. That amounted to half the cost of running the Centre each year. The other half was met by charges to groups, support from TVS, contributions from other Authorities and by an active fundraising campaign.

With the demise of ILEA this left a really big gap in the finances and the Centre began to run into debt. A vigorous fundraising programme was started to bridge this gap. It included an annual Open Day, making appeals to the Education Authorities now running the London Schools, and applications for sponsorship to banks, industry, Hampshire LEA and Charitable Trusts. This had fairly limited results and there was real concern about its future.

Meanwhile, the Countryside Education Trust was offering day visitor facilities for a wide range of environmental and countryside courses throughout the Beaulieu Estate. It was receiving support from Hampshire Education Authority, also from Esso, other local industries and a number of Charitable Trusts. Clearly two educational initiatives, both based on the Beaulieu Estate and both seeking funding from the same sources was going to present problems. In 1990, when this crisis arose, the CET was managing to balance its books, but not without considerable fundraising effort. Any competition for funds in the local area was certain to have a negative effect. If the OTC could not raise the support it needed outside the local area as it had in the past, it was quite possible that both organisations could fail. It was, therefore, imperative that a merger should be considered.

 It was not immediately obvious how the combined organisation would work. The OTC was set up as a not-for-profit charitable company under the guidance of ILEA. It was run by Governors and its aim was to provide an exciting and innovative farming and countryside experience for inner city children aged 8 - 13. Its educational work was based on its own site, Home Farm, other local farms, and the New Forest area. The CET, on the other hand, was a Charitable Trust providing a wide range of countryside and environmental education to school children of all ages from groups of toddlers to the most elderly adults who felt able to take part. It drew on the vast resources of the Beaulieu Estate, the New Forest and all the surrounding habitats, industrial opportunities, and even those outside the area or abroad. There were many problems to be overcome, but there was enormous commitment to ensuring that both projects survived and thrived into the future so that both children and adults could continue to benefit from the exceptional educational opportunities provided.

With the demise of ILEA and the uncertainty engendered, the bookings for the Out of Town Centre had dropped off alarmingly and the finances were deteriorating by the day. The whole situation was made even more urgent when the Company Secretary and Accountants had to advise the Governors of the Out of Town Country Pursuits Centre Ltd that the debt was such that under company law they were obliged to cease trading. So it was on 1st October 1991 that the OTC became part of the Countryside Education Trust, with all the problems and difficulties that entailed.

Graham Carter, as Director of the CET, was given the task of merging the Out of Town residential centre into the Trust. The Warden of the Centre, Dave Robinson, unfortunately had to be made redundant leaving the Centre with no resident warden on site. Staff of the CET had to take on responsibility for teaching residential groups at the

OTC, as well as day groups at the Woodland Study Centre, and there had to be major changes in work patterns and responsibilities for other staff. It was a difficult time for everybody.

The Centre itself needed to be refurbished if it was to appeal to a wider market, including older children and adults, and bookings needed to be increased within a very short period of time. So finance for refurbishment was the first major fundraising effort. Graham achieved this remarkably quickly and used the funds to introduce more modern features, particularly in the bedrooms and the main dining and recreational area. The tables and chairs, designed for the use of children, had to be replaced with adult sized furniture and the flooring replaced throughout. However, finance continued to be a major concern and raising sufficient income to cover running costs was a real problem.

The next imperative was to re-market the Centre offering the farming experience, and all the courses and facilities offered by the Trust, to the whole student age range. Schools who had used the Centre in the past were circulated with details of the changes. Advertisements were placed in educational and tourist publications and new leaflets were produced. Adult courses were planned, and holiday weeks and weekends were advertised to all groups who might take up the opportunity of staying at the Centre.

Work Goes On

Meanwhile, work at the Woodland Study Centre continued. The roof of the classroom had been leaking badly and it had to be re-felted. This was paid for by Fundraising Committee funds. Additional classroom space for visiting groups had become an urgent need and an additional building had been donated to the CET by Esso. It was a sectional building that had been on Esso's Fawley site and funds had already been raised for foundations and for the transfer of the building from Fawley to Hartford Wood. It would be positioned alongside and behind the existing WSC classroom and replace the caravan, which by this time was in poor condition anyway. Other sheds and the aviary would also go so that the site would be much improved by the additional building.

The number of visiting school groups to the WSC had reached an all time high in 1991 with 7476 day students taught by CET staff. Charges for services had been introduced the previous year and were now increased so it was encouraging to see that this had not deterred visitors. With the new commitment of teaching staff to the residential groups it was necessary to appoint a Seasonal Education Officer for the summer term to meet the demand. This was covered by the increased charges and the extra students taught. Despite the additional work load for all teaching staff, new courses continued to be developed for all ages and were taken up enthusiastically by visiting groups.

The Community Programme was going well and the new facilities available at the OTC were giving opportunity for residential courses for the first time. Holiday activities quickly booked up. The teenage ones were particularly ambitious and included a cycling trip in France based on an environmental education centre, La Maison de la Nature, just outside Caen. Art courses, Beaulieu River Boat Trips and a plant course were also offered. A very active volunteer group was doing work at both Hartford Wood and the OTC. In 1992 some adjustments to staffing were made. The fund-raiser's contract was terminated and the farm labourer was made redundant to reduce staff costs. The OTC secretary resigned and the Trust Administrator, Rosalyn Reed, became full-time to cover the work load. Alison Staples, Education Officer, left towards the end of

1992 and was not replaced until the following February in order to save money. There was also much discussion about how to reduce the deficit on the farm operation, which was proving to be a heavy financial burden.

In 1993 things began to improve. Bookings at the Out of Town Centre increased from 20 to 30 weeks and 11 weekends. Farm income improved with an increase to the size of the suckler herd producing about 70 calves to sell that year. Day visitor numbers continued to rise and Neil Jones was appointed as the new Education Officer, with Kate Dale as Summer Seasonal Education Officer. Elaine Knight helped with the day bookings on the farm.

The Victorian Christmas activity at Palace House showed a satisfactory profit and filled otherwise unpopular weeks for booking. Fund-raising was successful and some of the money borrowed from MVL was repaid. Everyone heaved a collective sigh of relief and staff were thanked for their efforts.

A new Government initiative was introduced that year to help those that were unemployed. Once again the CET applied for staff under the scheme. 'GrandMet', as it was called, eventually supplied 7 builders, 2 carpenters, 2 countryside rangers and 1 designer with a supervisor to ensure that work was carried out as required.

Also in 1993, for the first time, the CET benefitted from the introduction of a computer. It is almost impossible, now, to imagine how the work was done without a computer. It was difficult for staff at first. They all needed some training in how to use it, and some had never used a computer before. However, it soon came into its own and became a real asset to the organisation.

Fundraising continued to be a major and successful activity. Graham was able to obtain a number of grants and Lady Montagu and the Fund-raising Committee organised several events. The Trustees also raised money from their contacts. Margaret Carter raised over £500 by doing a cycle ride, and more money borrowed from MVL was paid back. Offering livery for two horses on the farm was another means of increasing income, but it did mean two stables were occupied in the winter when they were needed for the farm's own animals..

Despite concern over funds the CET did not stand still. Refurbishment continued in the residential centre, and work on the farmyard and Victorian looseboxes was carried out. Materials were obtained for some of the repairs from a wooden chalet bungalow that was donated to the Trust by Mr Peter Rogers of Fulmans, Beaulieu. The donation also included some furniture that was useful. The new building from Esso was installed at the wood and workers under the GandMet scheme provided invaluable assistance under the leadership of Alan Swan, a retired Army Colonel.

The extra groups being taught at the OTC did slightly reduce the number of day visit groups that could be taught. Also Philip Blandford had to leave quite suddenly in June making it necessary for Mike Shrubsole to take on extra duties with the residential groups. Kate Dale was asked to stay on as Education Officer when her seasonal post finished and a temporary Education Officer filled the gap.

The Community Programme continued to offer exciting and innovative courses. Teenagers took part in a 'Mountain Biking in Dorset' holiday and a 'French Cycling Holiday', both of which were very much enjoyed. These would be difficult to organise in the 21st century now that health and safety concerns have become so restrictive. There was also a French

exchange for young people. Adults and families benefitted from several courses run by Ray Mears who proved to be a very engaging and knowledgeable leader. There were also art courses, a dawn chorus and other birdwatching activities, boat trips, woodcraft and a National Bike Ride Day. For children 6-13 years there were Holiday Activities called 'I Love My Planet' which encouraged children to help take better care of our planet, a subject very dear to Viv Drake's heart, and one which we have all come to realise is essential if we are to continue to enjoy our world. These are just a sample of the courses run in a very successful year.

As a means of promoting the residential courses at the Out of Town Centre three free teachers weekends were organised. These required a

great deal of commitment of time and energy by all the staff, but they all took part with great enthusiasm. Teachers arrived on Friday evening and were given an interesting programme of talks and activities that gave them a real insight into the work of the CET and what opportunities were available to schools. The feed-back confirmed that all the teachers really enjoyed and appreciated their visits. The profile of the Trust was raised and the resulting bookings made it very worthwhile.

In April 1994 came the opening of the new building at the Woodland Study Centre, donated by Esso. It provided a second large classroom and valuable storage space for teaching materials. It was opened on 15th April by the Education Secretary Baroness Blatch. It was a real challenge to have paths laid and the site tidy for the event. This was made more difficult because part of the redevelopment programme had been to re-dig and contour the pond outside the WSC to provide additional pond dipping facilities, particularly for younger children. The operation had been planned for earlier in the year, but a delay resulted in it being finished only days before the opening event. Staff and Trustees really threw themselves into the task of making all ready for the important visitors and the day was a great success. The building was officially opened and in the evening an enthusiastic group of teachers attended an open evening to see the new building and all the extra facilities that would be available to them and their pupils.

Butterfly conservation was always a topic of interest to staff of the CET and many projects were undertaken to improve the woodland environment for their benefit, so it was with great delight that a special gift was received. Four brothers had carefully collected and preserved specimens of every type of moth and butterfly found in the UK since the beginning of the 20th Century, and the last surviving brother was looking for an organisation that would benefit from the collection. It came in an attractive mahogany case and was donated to the CET for use with groups visiting the WSC.

During the summer a Seasonal Education Officer was recruited from America. There was also a visit from a Forest Ranger from Zanzibar so the CET was truly international. In the Autumn Mike Shrubsole moved on after 7 years with the Trust, and Neil Jones took a teaching post in London. These were replaced by Andrea Kidd and Glynne Steele who, with Kate Dale made up the educational staff.

In October there was a lecture and a children's event given by David Shepherd. 180 children attended their event, while the lecture theatre was booked to capacity with 216 tickets sold for the adult talk. The takings were shared with the David Shepherd Conservation Foundation and both organisations benefitted.

1995 - 1996

By March 1995 the CET had made great progress. The residential centre had been full to capacity for the previous year, day bookings had remained at maximum during the summer term and satisfactorily high for the spring and autumn terms. All this activity, together with successful fund-raising efforts, resulted in a very encouraging positive balance at the bank. At last some more of the planned capital projects could be put in hand. One major need was new offices. Until this time the old office at the WSC had been used for all administration and it really was no longer adequate for all the work needed and was putting a great

strain on staff. The proposal was to convert the old Victorian pig sty building and deep litter chicken house at the OTC, into offices and classroom. This would bring the staff of the two centres into a closer working relationship as well as providing a much needed teaching space for day visitors to the farm. Other projects planned for the year were the replacement of the farm vehicle and the introduction of an adventure playground for the use of residential and day visitors to the OTC site.

A new venture for 1995 was the introduction of a Parent and Toddler Club. The idea was to give young children and their parents the opportunity to experience the great outdoors with an educational programme designed to increase their enjoyment and knowledge of the natural world. This ran on a once a month basis and was immediately popular. The first half-day meeting in February attracted 29 people and in March both a morning and afternoon session was required to meet the demand. This has continued to be extremely popular. Art courses led by Helen Talbot and Melvyn Gates were another innovation that proved to be very successful, and several Beaulieu River Boat Trips were booked to capacity.

The GrandMet scheme continued to supply very useful additional staff. An artist, Colin Brown, painted the inside of the new Esso classroom to show three different habitats in the New Forest, and a photographer, George Gammer, made an excellent promotional video for the OTC. Other staff did practical work around the WSC and the farm, but changes in Government policy terminated this scheme towards the end of the year.

All staff made visits to other centres in the area including Minstead Study Centre, Manor Farm, Stubbington, Foxleigh's Training Centre and Avon Tyrrell. This gave them the opportunity to see how other centres were run and develop new ideas for the CET. Everyone benefitted enormously from these visits. New ideas were developed and it helped to encourage the closer working relationship of the team.

During the rest of the year new topics were developed for the farm, and farm days were advertised. These proved popular, particularly a World War Two theme entitled 'Dig for Victory', which was great fun as well as very educational and fitted in with the requirements of the National Curriculum. Other interesting new courses included Tudors and Stuarts, Victorian Agriculture, and New Forest Commoning. These were advertised by a beautifully illustrated newsletter sent to all schools within reasonable travelling distance of the centre. Many responded to this mailing and bookings at both the

OTC and WSC (now renamed the New Forest Study Centre - NFSC) were very buoyant requiring a Seasonal Education Officer, Ruth Welch, and two sessional staff to help with day bookings and holiay activities. Kate suggested that it would be helpful to both the student and the organisation if the CET offered a year's work experience to a placement student from university for the following academic year. This was agreed, and Karen Tate from the University of Hertfordshire started her year in September 1995.

The farm did not flourish quite so well that year as wet weather early in the year followed by an exceptionally dry summer made life really difficult for Charlie. Grass and crops did not grow as they should, which left the animals short of feed. Extra pasture had to be purchased near Salisbury and the sheep transported to it. The grass did not grow enough for hay or silage to be made until really late in the year which left a substantial shortfall on winter feed that would have to be bought at additional expense. However, a replacement Landrover and a new fore-loader for the tractor were purchased and farm staff worked really hard to make the best of the situation.

At the OTC the Poultry House, at the back of the pig sties, was at last converted into new offices, which gave the staff the much better working conditions that they needed and the Victorian pig sties were converted into an interesting classroom for visiting groups. This came to be known as the Pig Sty Classroom much to the confusion or amusement of visiting groups.

The minibus owned by the CET at that time was a crew bus with side facing seats. After a serious accident on one of the nation's motorways, much concern was expressed that this was no longer safe enough for transporting children, so it was decided that it must be replaced. Hants CC made a welcome donation of £5,000 and Ford provided a silver, 17 seat minibus for that sum. It was clearly worth considerably more than that so they effectively made a donation of approximately £9,000, which was very much appreciated. Many groups were transported to off-site activities. Two popular studies were Bucklers Hard, and a stream study starting on the Hartford Heath. In order to ensure that all staff driving the minibus were doing so as safely as possible, a minibus trainer was appointed from the staff of the Motor Museum. Anyone driving the bus was required to hold a MIDAS (minibus driver awareness scheme) certificate from that time onwards.

Bookings continued to be high throughout 1995 with 43 residential weeks and 21 weekends booked at the OTC. As this level of booking was clearly going to continue into 1996 it was decided to make Ruth a permanent member of staff bringing the number up to four Education Officers. Other staff changes saw Simon Farr replacing Kate, now Kate Cheng since her marriage during the year. This did place an extra financial burden on the Trust but it had been the best financial year since the foundation of the CET. The loan was repaid to MVL, and with the extra bookings at both centres and the continuing support from Hampshire County Council it was possible to look forward to real developments in services and capital projects.

The Community Programme continued to attract large numbers in 1996. The Little Owls parent and toddler group went from strength to strength. Teenagers were able to take part in a South Downs Walking Holiday and a Dorset Cycling Trip. The Summer Holiday Activities included a Wild Wood camping challenge for 11 -13 year olds and an imaginative programme for 6 - 11 year olds to explore their different senses. A fully booked debate with Jonathan Porritt early in the year was followed later by Chris Packham filling the lecture theatre for a talk on badgers and other New Forest wildlife. This was in addition to a great range of smaller talks, walks and boat trips.

Hartford Stream, rising on Hartford Heath and running down through the Estate to the estuary of the Beaulieu River has always been important for groups doing studies on fresh-water ecology, but over the years the whole valley had become choked with rhododendron. Many groups had been organised to cut back the growth but rhododendron returns very quickly unless it is treated with herbicide. In 1996, Viv managed to obtain a grant for this treatment and to help with the ongoing work of cutting back the bushes in order to restore the valley mire. Gradually this work paid off and the valley was much restored to an open habitat with native plants and bushes coming back.

Changes in Local Government resulted in the formation of Southampton and Portsmouth Unitary Authorities. As a result the CET had to negotiate with Hants CC plus Southampton and Portsmouth councils in order to obtain Local Government grants. This made a great deal more work for Graham and Ros and caused considerable anxiety, although in the end all three Authorities agreed to continue to support the work of the Trust.

There were a number of changes of staff towards the end of 1996 and the beginning of 1997. Leon Gale was appointed to help on the farm and he soon helped to improve farm presentation. Andrea Kidd and Glynne Steel left at the end of August 1996 and were replaced by Tamsin Bent. Ruth Welch left early in 1997, leaving Simon Farr and Tamsin Bent to manage the educational programme with the help of Lucy Attwood who was one of the current placement students from the University of Hertfordshire. They were joined by Angus Reid, and Alison Groves as Seasonal Education Officers, for the summer of 1997. The other one year placement student, Adrian Lee, was helping Viv Drake with the Community Programme. Simon Hayes was employed to improve maintenance on the OTC site and made an excellent job of rebuilding the steps on the path leading up to Moonhills.

At the Trustees meeting in July it was recorded that the bookings at the OTC for the year 97/98 were excellent, and that the year 98/99 was already half booked. Bookings at the NFSC were so high the situation even gave rise to some concern being expressed that the habitat would be damaged if any more groups were taken! An Ofsted Report carried out by Tony Pearce gave a glowing picture of the services provided by the CET so everybody involved in the organisation could be justifiably pleased with the progress made.

1997 - Building the Cob Cottage

An exciting project was planned for the summer of 1997. There had been a suggestion that it would be good to build a cob cottage for the CET. History suggested that one way that a family could obtain living accommodation was if they created it themselves on a piece of Forest land. This was not allowed by law, and if they were caught building a house it would be pulled down. However, if they constructed it really quickly and had a fire burning in the hearth then it was a dwelling and the law enforcement officers were not

allowed to touch it. The legend said that local villagers would band together, collect the materials so they would be all ready, and then at a suitable time they would start early and aim to have a cottage built in a single day. Well this was a theory that just had to be tested.

Bob Bennett of the Lime Centre near Winchester and a friend, Trevor Innes, were keen to try this out and had been looking for somewhere to do it where it would be useful for educational purposes. Their enthusiasm had caught the imagination of Graham Carter, Viv Drake and the Trustees of the CET as far back as 1995 and work was started to make this happen on the Beaulieu Estate. A possible site was identified in Hartford Wood, planning permission was obtained, and funds were raised. To make it more interesting it was suggested that it should be done in period costume and set in 1650, and that there should be a story to go with it. So the plan progressed and it was decided that the people of the fictional village would be getting together to build a cottage for a young couple who wanted to get married and, if they were successful, the couple would move in straight away, establish it as a home and be safe from the law enforcement officers.

In order for all this to be achieved volunteers and staff would have to become the villagers and be prepared for a day of very hard work. As it happened this did not prove to be as difficult as might be expected. Lots of people loved the idea of taking part in such an adventurous project, and before long there were over a hundred people involved. All these had to be dressed in appropriate costumes and hats to play the part, all of which had to be made. Jill Fry was a real treasure and with a team of helpers created most of the costumes needed. Tools and wheelbarrows had to be created in the appropriate style and there had to be days of practice

so that the cob material used for the construction would hold together. Carpenters would be needed to construct the roof timbers, door, windows and ladders so that thatchers could finish the roof and make it water-tight.

Finally all was ready and on 21st June 1997 the day came to build the 'House in Time'!
It had been very wet in the weeks leading up to the day and the site was very muddy, but that did not deter the workers. At 3.30am they began

to congregate in Hartford Wood and at first light at 4.00 am the group wound their way through the wood to

the site. The cameras of the Meridian TV camera crew began to roll and the work began. There were those who mixed the clay and straw and teams who laid it for the walls and trampled it down. Whole families took part with children just as keen to become 'wall walkers' as their parents. While they were doing the

walls the carpenters put the roof beams together and cooks prepared authentic 17th century food. There was a blacksmith on site making the door and window furniture, and later a pig began to roast. By early afternoon the walls were built the roof was on and the twelve skilled thatchers began their task.

For some time there was concern that it would not be finished before nightfall, but at 9.20pm, just as the light

was failing, the last piece of thatch was put into place and the celebration could begin. The young couple were married by the friar and the dancing began accompanied by traditional mediaeval players. The food was wonderful, the pig was roasted perfectly and wine and cider flowed. Everyone was exhausted but the cottage was complete and it was declared a monumental success.

Many people had visited the site during the day to watch the work in progress, and it was made a major feature on the Meridian TV news. Later a video and book were made of the whole day. Many people were fascinated by the story of how a cob cottage - 'The House in Time' - could be built in one day and they

were eager to buy copies of the book and video, especially those who had been involved

in building it. Schools were also interested in acquiring copies, particularly those who visited the site and were studying Tudors as part of their school curriculum.

Further work was needed on the cob cottage and surrounding site, and there was much help from volunteers who had been involved in the project. They had to ensure that any cracking of the cob material as it dried out was repaired and that lime wash was applied to the building to protect it. Also there was need of more drainage for the site which required much digging and moving of materials. All their work and enthusiasm was of enormous value to the CET, they had really taken the building to their hearts.

During late summer that year the new adventure style play area, called Trail Blazers, was installed at the Out of Town Centre, made possible by a £20,000 grant. This was much appreciated by all visitors to the site, but particularly by residential groups who really enjoyed the outside space afforded by the patio, play area and now the playground. As about 80% of residential visitors were from inner city areas these presented great freedom for them.

There was much disappointment later in the year when fundraising applications were refused. One was for the refurbishment and development of the Beaulieu Tide Mill. This had been a major feature in the wish list of

the Montagu family, Graham Carter and the Trustees of the CET and was a bitter disappointment, particularly as it had looked as if it might be achieved at last.

The other application refused was to the National Lottery for development of the Out of Town Centre site to include a car park and other much needed facilities. Fundraising applications were taking a lot of staff time and it was frustrating as well as disappointing when these were turned down.

Staff training and development days continued to be considered of real importance to ensure that staff remained full of fresh ideas. Visits were made to many other centres including Bramley Frith, Minstead Study Centre, farm centres, and Bore Place where staff learnt to use a pole lathe. There was also

First Aid training and MIDAS certificates needed to be renewed. Staff were encouraged to be a part of the Hampshire Environmental Education Group (HEEG) in order to make friends with staff from all the other educational centres. Activities were discussed with the Calshot Activity Centre and some joint ventures were planned. Staff were sent on courses and training days and the Trust benefitted enormously from them bringing in new ideas and enthusiasm. The New Forest Show became a place where great networking took place. Viv Drake found it particularly useful as she often found interesting people there who would lead some of the community courses that she planned and, of course, it was a wonderful opportunity to raise awareness of the CET and its work.

1998 - The CET Garden

One exciting project for 1998 concerned the north end of the Out of Town Centre site. For several years a new garden had been planned for the OTC but it had been hampered by lack of funds and an enormous heap of subsoil that had been left when the residential centre foundations had been dug. A number of grants had been received for the work and it was now possible to go ahead. First the heap of sub-soil was removed, then plans were drawn up by Simon Farr and a date was set for a volunteer weekend called the 'Trowels of Life'. Hampshire County Council awarded a grant while plants, drainage materials and soil improver were offered by local companies. So on the 4th and 5th April 1998 staff and volunteers assembled for the volunteer weekend in which it was hoped that real progress would be made. The weather was awful. The ground was so wet that it was like working in a lake and everyone was soon soaked to the skin, but no one was going to let it stop them. By the end of the weekend paths had been laid, raised gardens and ponds had been constructed and

filled with soil and there was a real sense of achievement. A second volunteer weekend saw further progress and a straw bale shed was constructed in which to keep tools and other equipment.

The Little Owls parent and toddler club, providing 2 session on one day per month, had become so popular that it was decided to run 2 days each month. Other community activities were also continuing to be popular with film evenings, art events, and music and song led by Stan Seaman and Friends. Holiday Activities continued to be innovative and well booked up. The farm, however, was of more concern. The Charity Commission was insisting that more detailed records must be kept of all animals on the farm, those that were born, died, bought and sold. If this was not done accurately the consequences would be extremely serious. It has never been easy to make a small mixed farm pay its way and with the additional demands for its educational use it had continued to be impossible to make the books balance. However, the farm had always made such a significant contribution to the experience of visitors to the OTC that every effort needed to

be made to improve its presentation, management and accessibility so that it could be used in a way that increased the income generated and made it available to a wider range of visitors. It was decided that to reduce the size of the farm would reduce losses, so the land at Moonhills was surrendered back to the estate. Angus Reid was appointed Farm Interpretive Officer, under the NLCB grant, in order to progress ideas for farm improvement and marketing. Lucy Attwood was appointed to replace Angus as Education Officer joining Simon Farr and Tamsin Bent.

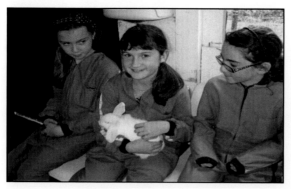

There were other staff changes in 1998. Rosalyn Reed was appointed Trust Administrator in order to take some of the pressure off Graham. This made her the senior member of staff on site with responsibility for administration, staff, volunteers and site maintenance. To help her with this additional work, Jenny O'Dell was appointed as half-time secretary.

There was tremendous excitement when the NLCB made a grant of £188,199 to the CET. This was to fund 3 staff - an Environmental Policy Officer, a Farm Interpretive

Officer and a Farm Assistant. It would also pay for a car park, toilet block, and fencing and improvements to the farm site for day visitors. Projects, that had been planned for ages, could now be carried out. The part of the money to encourage the environmental development of the site led to the appointment of Laura Bulteel. She was to assist Viv Drake in achieving this. She and Viv undertook an environmental survey and started to introduce a number of cost saving measures. Solar panels were installed on the roof of the OTC to provide hot water for the centre, water-butts were installed around the buildings making rainwater available for garden and farm use, and a 'Rocket' composter was introduced that would recycle food waste from the OTC into compost that could be used on the vegetable gardens. Everyone was encouraged to think of ways in which they could be more sensitive to saving money, energy and water and this resulted in a saving of over £2,000. Many other new teaching initiatives, energy saving ideas and environmentally friendly projects also became a reality. The new car park was laid, and a new toilet block was built at the end of the residential building. This had been needed for day visitors for a long time and it made it possible for the old Portacabin type toilet block that had stood in the garden to be removed. All these improvements transformed the approach to the residential centre, and visitors and coaches had room to park and maneuver as never before.

1999

In early 1999 Angus Reid moved on and Simon Hayes moved to the position of Farm Interpreter. Barry Marcer was employed to cover maintenance. A new government scheme for the unemployed was introduced now called 'New Deal'. This provided a team of a supervisor and 9 workers. They became a significant part of the workforce and carried out many development and maintenance projects. The area inside and outside the Miracle Span was concreted and the workshop moved from its former position in the middle of the farmyard to the Miracle Span. The Victorian looseboxes were improved and painted. Four chicken pens were created with six foot fencing so the laying hens could have outside space protected from foxes. New pigsties were built giving better accommodation for the pigs and easier access for children. A path was laid along the bank between the lower paddocks and the orchard, and fencing and steps around the site were improved.

The OTC garden made further significant progress with live willow fencing at the front, a butterfly garden, a vegetable garden and polytunnel. The area where the toilet cabin had stood was also redesigned. A group from MIND was involved with the cultivation and courses on gardening were developed. However, Simon Farr moved on to a new job in September, which left the garden half completed. Ros, who had always been interested in the garden and had a lot of experience in this field, took over the guidance of the work.

A regular newsletter had been sent to both junior and secondary schools for several years by this time. This was clearly a very successful way of reminding schools of the many services on offer by the CET and showed in the increased bookings  of both day and residential visits following the mailings. Circulation of the 'SETOUT' leaflet through the New Forest Post and by distribution to libraries, Information Centres, schools and many other places resulted in increased bookings of community courses and a greater awareness of the CET in the area. As competition increased it became more and more important to ensure that the CET remained well known as an active part of the community with a constant flow of imaginative and interesting courses for both schools and the community at large.

One exciting course in May 1999 was to build a roundhouse in Hartford Wood by the New Forest Study Centre buildings. There had been need of extra shelter and teaching space for some time as there were often as many as 5 groups at the centre at lunchtimes in the summer months. This could prove very difficult if the weather was poor. Two or even three classes from the same school could be encouraged to eat lunch in one classroom with a bit of a squash, but with different schools on day visits, and students from the residential centre as well, the two classrooms were proving inadequate. The roundhouse also added another dimension to the teaching programme so it was a great success in every way.

Other community courses included a Back in Time film evening, a Badger Night, Guided Walks based on the Beaulieu and Sowley Estates looking at the influence of the Cistercian Monks, and a summer Cycle Ride planned to coincide with National Bike Week. For the Friends of the Trust, a Barn Dance took place at Beufre Barn in June. As well as preparing the community programme, Viv did a great deal of fundraising to make many projects possible, which was an enormous help to the ongoing work of the Trust.

Earth Education became very popular at this time and Lucy and Laura became very interested in it. They attended courses and shared experiences with other groups and set up an Advanced Leadership course which was held at the New Forest Study Centre in July. This was well attended and lead to the introduction of yet more courses that would be interesting for the many visitors. The new numeracy and literacy programme introduced into schools provided another challenge requiring new ways of addressing these issues within the programme of the CET. Other educational activities were explored through the Summer Holiday Activities with a Week on the Wild Side for 6 - 10 year olds and a Week on the Wilder Side for 11 - 13 year olds which included an overnight survival camp and the use of maps and compasses. Much fun was had by all who attended.

The CET was asked to take part in a new project for the Motor Museum. The plan was to set up a Family Farm area in the orchard in the middle of the Motor Museum site. This would increase the range of attractions for their young visitors and it was felt that staff of the CET had the necessary expertise to help with it. This did involve a great deal of work for the CET, particularly the farm staff, as they constructed fences and houses for the animals. This rather delayed work at the OTC, but it was good to co-operate with Beaulieu staff and establish closer working relations.

The Millenium and the End of an Era

The year 2000 was a great milestone for everyone. Early in the year it was decided that Graham Carter, who had been suffering from increasingly severe ill health for some time, would retire from his position as Director of the CET at the end of the year. He had continued to give his services to the CET on a part-time basis throughout the years while acting as Director of Education at the Motor Museum, but it was felt that the time had come for a full-time Trust Manager to be appointed. Initially he/she would serve as Education Officer under Graham's guidance taking full duties as Manager on 1st January 2001. From that time Alex Glanville, who was Land Agent for the Beaulieu Estate, would act as senior officer for the CET to support the new Manager and be accountable to the Trustees. This didn't quite work out as planned as no suitable candidate was found to replace Graham during the year and much greater responsibility had to be taken by Ros as Trust Administrator.

Despite every effort to improve the situation, it was clear that the farm was continuing to lose money and that the larger it was the more money it cost the Trust. It was decided that it could provide an interesting and exciting experience for all visitors with fewer animals and much less land. So the farm was reduced to 12 acres, the number of animals was also reduced and after 20 years service Charlie Knight had to move on to other things. However, in April the plans to open the farm to the public on one day per week came into operation under the

guidance of Simon Hayes. This also marked the 25th Anniversary of the CET and there were great hopes that this would encourage local people to visit and become more involved with the centre, as well as bringing in much needed funds

After 14 years, a grant from Esso, that supported the work of the Community Officer came to an end. Their support had been invaluable and was much missed. Graham and Viv both increased their fundraising efforts in an attempt to replace the funds. All agreed that the community programme was a really important part of the CET as it was all inclusive, attracted national funding, promoted families working together and offered a unique programme. It was far too important to lose.

In February there was a free weekend for leaders of youth groups to introduce them to what the CET had to offer. The CET pickup had to be replaced and a Landrover was purchased for use on the farm. A van that had been used by the maintenance staff at Beaulieu was also purchased in order to move equipment around the sites to save using, and possibly damaging the minibus.

The new CET website came on-line making it possible for schools to contact the Trust more readily. Jez Hailwood replaced Laura Bulteel as Sustainability Officer and had great talent with computers. This proved invaluable in managing the website.

The garden continued to progress under Ros's guidance and in May a lych gate was installed at the entrance. This was made by apprentices learning their craft at Vosper Thornicroft's shipyard in Southampton. It made a very impressive addition to the garden and gave it a feeling that visitors had arrived somewhere special.

A charcoal earthburn took place in the summer led by Alan Walters who worked at the Weald and Downland Open Air Museum. In the early days of the Trust there had been an attempt to set up a charcoal burner's camp and there had always been an interest in demonstrating how charcoal was traditionally made. The burn took place as a weekend course and Open Day and included an iron smelting demonstrated by Jake Keen, and a variety of woodland crafts including pole-lathe turning, hurdle making and wood carving, all taking place in Bakers Meadow in Hartford Wood. It was well attended and created much interest among local people and those from further afield.

Ralph Montagu

The most pressing task for the CET was to appoint a new Manager and another Education Officer to start in September as Lucy Attwood and Beth Stone would be unable to manage once the Student placement had left at the end of August. Advertisements were duly placed in CJS (Countryside Job Service) and the Educational Guardian. This led to the appointment of Alison Charters as the Education Officer but, again, there appeared to be no suitable candidates for the position of Manager. Lord Montagu resigned as Chair of the Trustees and Ralph Montagu took his place. Alex Glanville was confirmed as the new Director to start on 1st January 2001 and he and Ralph prepared 'A Plan for the 21st Century' so that the work would be guided into the future.

SetOut
September – December 2005
CONNECT WITH THE COUNTRYSIDE

An informal illustrated talk by TV wildlife presenter Chris Packham about some of the New Forest's most glamorous plants and animals!

Friday 16th December
7.30pm – 9.30pm
in the National Motor Museum lecture theatre, Beaulieu
Tickets: £5.50 per adult & £3.00 per child (up to 16yrs), Friends of the Trust £5.00/£2.50

A great pre-Christmas event for families

Early booking is strongly recommended

This is a joint event with the New Forest Badger Group

Chris Packham
Presents Wildlife of the New Forest

MUD, MUD, Glorious MUD!

Woodland Open Day & BBQ

Come and help us daub the walls of our newly built roundhouse at the New Forest Study Centre, Beaulieu

Thursday 27th October 10.00am – 4.00pm

Daubing with a mud and straw mix will protect the hazel wattle and strengthen the whole structure so that the roundhouse should last for a good number of years.

Entrance: £2.50 per adult, £1.50 per child, Friends of the Trust £2.00/£1.00 (please bring your membership card). No need to book - just turn up!

Parking: Hides Field, National Motor Museum. Follow signs marked Woodland Open Day. From Hides Field, it is a short walk to the New Forest Study Centre. Suitable for buggies/pushchairs. Wheelchair users, please call us so that we can help. The event will take place whatever the weather! The woods are sheltered and there is plenty of indoor space.

If you'd like to take part, just turn up and bring some old clothes to wear!
Other activities:

- Woodland walks
- Games & activities for children
- Toddler trail
- Living history in our cob house
- Mud oven bread and cake making
- Countryside crafts
- BBQ – locally produced food
- Homemade cakes, teas and coffees

BOOK NOW
To book events tel: **01590 612401** or e-mail: [
(Leave your name, address, tel number and which events you
We'll reserve your place/s. Then send in your payment and we'll return all the nece
for up to one week. **BY LETTER:** Just send in your payment with a note to say wh
as soon as possible. Cheques are payable to 'Countryside Education Trust'. Adva

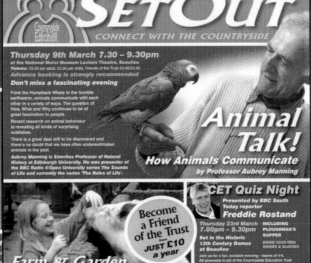

SetOut
January – April 2006
CONNECT WITH THE COUNTRYSIDE

Thursday 9th March 7.30 – 9.30pm
at the National Motor Museum Lecture Theatre, Beaulieu
Tickets: £5.50 per adult, £3.00 per child, Friends of the Trust £5.00/£2.50
Advance booking is strongly recommended

Don't miss a fascinating evening

From the Humpback Whale to the humble earthworm, animals communicate with each other in a variety of ways. The question of How, What and Why continues to be of great fascination to people.

Recent research on animal behaviour is revealing all kinds of surprising subtleties.

There is a great deal still to be discovered and there's no doubt that we have often underestimated animals in the past.

Aubrey Manning is Emeritus Professor of Natural History at Edinburgh University. He was presenter of the BBC Radio 4/Open University series The Sounds of Life and currently the series 'The Rules of Life'.

Animal Talk!
How Animals Communicate
by Professor Aubrey Manning

Become a Friend of the Trust from JUST **£10** a year

CET Quiz Night
Presented by BBC South Today reporter
Freddie Rostand

Thursday 23rd March
7.00pm – 9.30pm
INCLUDING PLOUGHMAN'S SUPPER
Set in the Historic 13th Century Domus at Beaulieu
BRING YOUR OWN DRINKS & GLASSES

Join us for a fun, sociable evening – teams of 4-6.
All proceeds in aid of the Countryside Education Trust
COST: £5.00 per person including supper
BOOKING: Advance booking only. Book Early!

Farm & Garden OPEN DAY & BBQ

Thursday 6th April
10.00am – 4.00pm
at the Out of Town Centre, Beaulieu
Entrance: £3.00 per adult, £2.00 per child, Friends of the Trust £2.50/£1.50 (please bring your membership card).

NO NEED TO BOOK – JUST TURN UP!
FREE PARKING as directed opposite the Out of Town Centre

- Farm Animals
- Bread & Butter M[
- Wooden Sculpture
  activities for child
- 'Green' Footprint
- Pony & Trap Ride
- Hedgehogs
- Plant Sale
- Beekeeping Disp[
- Try Your Hand at [
- Refreshments – [
- BBQ – Local Prod[

INSIDE

BOOK NOW
To book events tel: 0159[
(Leave your name, address, tel number [
We'll reserve your place/s. Then send in your paym[
for up to one week. **BY LETTER:** Just send in your p[
soon as possible. Cheques are payable to 'Countrysi[

SetOut
September - December 2007
CONNECT WITH THE COUNTRYSIDE

'Stitching the world back into working order'

A lightning tour of the world of natural history with good news stories en route

by Professor David Bellamy OBE

Thursday 22nd November 7.30 - 9.30pm
in the lecture theatre of the National Motor Museum, Beaulieu

TICKETS: £6.00 per adult, £3.00 per child, Friends of the Trust £5.00/£2.50

APPLE OPEN DAY

Woodland Open Day
with an Apple Theme
Say Farewell to the old Study Centre
Thurs 25th Oct from 10am to 3.30pm
at New Forest Study Centre, Beaulieu

Entrance: £3 - adult, £2 - child
Friends of the Trust £2.50/£1.50 (with membership card)
NO NEED TO BOOK – JUST TURN UP
Parking: Follow signs from National Motor Museum entrance

- Farm animals & Pony & trap rides
- Tasting of over 20 unusual apple varieties
- Tasting of freshly pressed apple juices from hill farm products 80
- Talks on apple varieties by orchard expert Stan French.
- Pruning demonstration
- Archery competition with prizes (small charge of £1.00 for this activity)
- New forest cider tasting
- Apple & spoon race, apple bobbing & other fun games for children
- Cookery demonstration - apple recipes
- BBQ - locally produced food
- Homemade cakes & biscuits including apple recipes, teas & coffees

Whales, Dolphins and Sharks around Britain
Thursday 13th December 7.30 - 9.30pm
at the National Motor Museum lecture theatre

You don't have to travel to the other side of the world to view whales, dolphins and basking sharks. The waters around the west coast of Britain abound with a wonderful range of marine wildlife such as these and much more!
Find out what wildlife you might see in our waters in the company of marine naturalist Colin Speedie.
Colin Speedie has spent a lifetime on, in and under the sea in the waters around Britain as a commercial yachtmaster and wildlife researcher. For the last nine years he has led the Wildlife Trust's Basking Shark Project.

TICKETS: £6.00 per adult, £3.00 per child, Friends of the Trust and/or Hampshire Wildlife Trust £5.00/£2.50

Inside

Advanced booking & payment essential on all events (unless otherwise stated)

BOOK NOW
To book events Tel: **01590 612401** or e-mail: **mail@cet.org.uk**
(Leave your name, address, telephone number and which events you wish to book)
We'll reserve your place/s. Then send in your payment and we'll return all the necessary details. Reservations will be held for up to one week. **BY LETTER:** Just send in your payment with a note to say which events you wish to book and we'll confirm your booking as soon as possible. Cheques are payable to 'Countryside Education Trust'. Advance bookings are needed for all events unless specified.

Chapter 5

Countryside Education Trust 2001

2001 was the beginning of a new era for the CET. Alex Glanville was the new Director and plans were in hand to appoint a new Manager.

The Out of Town residential Centre was really well booked for the year, there were many day bookings for Hartford Wood and the community programme was continuing with exciting and innovative courses and events. The farm had settled to its new way of working under Elaine's guidance, so all looked set for a good year.

It appeared that the CET could run quite smoothly for a few months until the new Manager was in place, BUT on 18th February Foot and Mouth struck! It was very soon clear that this was not an isolated incident and it rapidly began to spread over the country. There were great pyres as animals were incinerated and every news report told of a worsening situation. Very soon the phone started to ring with worried teachers wondering if they should bring their children to a farm site. Was the CET still open for business and was

this a responsible decision to take? What was the CET doing to protect itself from infection? What would happen if Foot and Mouth broke out in the area, would the children be trapped on-site and not allowed to go home? The questions went on and on and Ros really felt in the hot seat. Some schools cancelled and some County Councils were advising schools not to take children to the countryside. It began to look as if this national crisis could have a very serious effect on the CET. By March cancellations had already cost the Trust over £18,000. Trustees stepped in to make decisions and Graham and Alex gave what support they could, but it was a very anxious time for everybody. Gradually the situation came under control and the pressure began to recede.

Meanwhile further advertisements had been placed and interviews took place for the new Manager. David Bridges was appointed to the post and took up the position in May. David came from a teaching background. He had been Senior Master at a Special School, but had most recently been running his own landscape gardening business so he was well qualified to take on the management of the CET. He had an office at the OTC so he was well positioned to know all that was happening within the organisation and the staff welcomed him and looked forward to working with him. Naturally many things changed and at the end of the year it was decided that, as David was carrying out many tasks that had been done by the Trust Administrator, Ros should reduce her hours to 4 days per week and that Jenny O'Dell should become PA to David.

During the summer of 2001 the CET was awarded a substantial grant by the Esmee Fairburn Foundation for the development of the Garden. This provided funds for a Gardener to be appointed for 3 years, for a large

greenhouse to be purchased and for the provision of tools, materials and equipment for the running of the Garden. With David's background in landscape gardening he was delighted and was encouraged by the Trustees to completely redesign the area. The new job was advertised and Ulrike Seydel was appointed as the Garden Education Officer to begin work in January 2002. A grant had also been received to build a Garden Room. This was to be an oak framed building with a shingle roof that would provide work space for groups whose courses were based in the Garden.

For the first time Summer Holiday Activities were not fully booked. Bookings had been coming in later and later in recent years, and times were changing. Many more centres in the area were offering holiday activities providing sports and interest themes and this was obviously having its effect. Much thought was given to what type of activities should be offered in the future.

The MIND Team continued to provide workers to help with maintenance tasks and projects and Chris Rogers was appointed as the new supervisor. Ros was asked to provide a work schedule for them.

Two training days were made available to staff. One was a day at Wisley that staff found very worthwhile and interesting. The other was a two day event called 'Rewarding Relationships' designed to help staff to relate well in the workplace and improve teamwork and effectiveness.

Jez Hailwood moved on at the end of September. He had worked very hard on the sustainability programme and contributed to the CET being awarded Eco-Centre status. Also he had been of invaluable help in setting up and maintaining the website for the Trust. He was very much missed, but continued to help with updating the website from his new position. New work placement students started in September. Andrew Cook was the new Assistant Community Officer and Jenny Stansbridge the Assistant Education Officer.

There was a very successful Open Day at the New Forest Study Centre that was well attended, but, despite considerable maintenance work having been done on the buildings over the previous two years, they were getting very shabby and the structure was deteriorating. On one occasion when one of the Education Officers had been teaching, the floor in the old building had given way beneath her. This greatly amused the children, but was rather disconcerting for the member of staff. This second hand building had served the Trust for 20 years and it looked very much as if it was coming to the end of its life. Another item that had caused concern was the sewage treatment plant at the wood. This had developed a leak which had to be repaired at considerable cost.

2002

During 2002 there was considerable improvement on the farm and a really good Open Day in April. The Garden Room was constructed, making a wonderful new teaching facility within the Garden. It was called the Isabel Herbert Garden Room in memory of Lady Montagu's mother who had done so much work for the Trust for many years. It was a very fitting memorial to a very gracious lady.

A large second hand greenhouse was bought and constructed and the new design for the Garden was taking shape under David's leadership. Esso made funds available to fit out the greenhouse providing modern metal staging for one half. In the other half deep beds were constructed for growing protected crops. The plan was to grow food crops from around the world.

In the summer a very high profile and prestigous event took place. Mark Knopfler, who lived locally, agreed to do a concert for the Trust. This was to be a grand fundraising occasion taking place within the grounds of the Motor Museum. There had been a yearly musical event for some years run by the Beaulieu Estate, called the Beaulieu Proms, so it seemed an ideal time to add an event for the CET while the stage, lighting and other structures were in place. It was incredibly successful and everyone who attended it really enjoyed the occasion.

Another summer event was the Estate Open Day. This was organised by the Countryside Foundation for Education in conjunction with the Beaulieu Estate and the CET. The idea was to encourage big landowners to show a variety of activities that take place on a country estate, or have been traditional crafts or activities in the country. The day took place in Hartford Wood and showed activities including making cleft fence posts, the work of the gamekeeper, and how timber was processed by sawing and chipping. There was also a

New Forest pony and a gun dog display. Then, with a more historic theme, visitors were shown how people would have lived in the cob cottage, and a pole lathe demonstration and talk was given. Schools, particularly those from inner cities, were invited to bring their children free of charge, and over 300 young students took part.

After the financial concern of the previous year it was felt that it was really important to set up a reserve fund that could be drawn upon in time of crisis. Obviously this couldn't be achieved all at once, but it was felt that with careful management of funds, a sum of £25,000 could be put aside. This would not only make the Trust more secure, but it would give it more credibility when applying for grants.

With the introduction of risk assessments it was felt that it was very important that in all areas of the work careful thought should be given to the risks involved. There had been very few accidents on any of the CET sites throughout its time of operation and it was important that visitors should know that there was a responsible attitude to Health and Safety. Many teachers and other group leaders were quite nervous of taking children out into the countryside. They had little experience themselves and increasingly relied on the staff of the centre to ensure the safety of their charges. All staff were asked to write risk assessments for their areas of responsibility, which was a very time consuming task, but very necessary as schools soon started asking for copies of these before they brought their groups to the centres.

The pig sty pens either side of the Pig Sty Classroom had proved to be rather unsatisfactory once the building had been converted. If they were left empty they gathered rubbish or equipment and looked untidy. If they were used for the smaller animals they didn't seem to thrive as the concrete floors got wet when it rained and they got too hot in the sun. The idea was put forward that the ones facing down the farmyard should be turned into a child sized rabbit warren. To make this possible Wessex Water was approached to supply suitable pipes which they donated and even cut to size and delivered. Wooden tunnels were then made to join the pipes together and the whole structure was covered in a woodchip, sand and cement mix and planted with sedums and other drought resistant plants. The children loved it immediately, and most groups spent many happy times playing in this new facility.

An interesting programme of events was provided under the Community Programme including an insect course, a pruning course, BBQ and walk at the NFSC, other estate walks, and boat trips. There was a grand Open Evening to mark the official opening of the Garden Room which was attended by Fred Dinenage.

Other Open Days were held at the OTC in April and at the NFSC in October. Both were well attended and enjoyed by all.

Later in the year David and Viv obtained a grant from the Community Fund for disadvantaged children from the surrounding area to have a free residential week at the Out of Town Centre. Local schools who had large numbers of children from poorer backgrounds would be invited to apply for one of the six weeks allocated. They would then be able to bring a class of children free of charge, paid for by the lottery grant. The scheme was to last for 3 years giving the chance for 18 school classes to take part in this unique opportunity. Viv also applied to Hampshire County Council for a grant from their 'Early Learning' scheme to encourage pre-school groups to take advantage of free visits to the CET. This was also successful.

A scheme called 'Investors in People' had been set up to give recognition to work places that encouraged their staff by giving training and opportunities in the workplace. The CET was the first employer on the Beaulieu Estate to be awarded this accreditation.

On 4th December the staff of the CET took part in the Beaulieu Village Victorian Christmas. It was great fun providing a nativity scene with live animals and suitable fancy dress for Mary, Joseph, shepherds and angels. CET staff also led carol singing and visitors to Beaulieu enthusiastically joined in.

The usual Victorian Christmas activities took place at Palace House during the last three weeks of term. These provided the opportunity for CET and Motor Museum staff to work together to give children a flavour of what it would have been like to live in Victorian times. Both children and staff dressed in appropriate costumes of the Victorian era and children went home more aware of how life was lived then. Staff were also glad to go home at the end of term for a much needed rest.

2003 - 2006

In 2003 Chris Rogers was appointed to do maintenance work on Mondays, Wednesdays and Fridays. He would continue as MIND team supervisor on the other days. This helped a lot as many repairs and practical projects had been delayed when there was no one to carry them out. The whole site soon started to look much better.

A visit was made in January to the Minstead Study Centre. This was much enjoyed by CET staff and everyone was made very welcome. Their buildings and facilities were much more limited than those available on the Beaulieu Estate, but there were lots of good ideas to share and it was a good opportunity for the staff of the two centres to get to know each other better.

There had been some break in the coppicing that had been carried out each winter for the 20 years up to 2000, but it was considered important to get this started again. This was not only to supply materials for the garden and other projects, but to continue to provide a range of habitats in the woodland. Many animals, plants and insects rely on the open areas and different heights of woodland growth provided by the regular cutting of the hazel stools. The bio-diversity of the woodland would be much poorer without it, so it was decided that every effort should be made to cut a half acre coup.

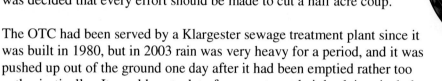

The OTC had been served by a Klargester sewage treatment plant since it was built in 1980, but in 2003 rain was very heavy for a period, and it was pushed up out of the ground one day after it had been emptied rather too enthusiastically. It would cost a lot of money to settle it back into its hole, and it had caused concern for some time. It had not been possible to connect to mains drainage in the early days as there was no sewage system close enough to access from the centre, but new drainage pipes laid down Beaulieu hill now made it feasible and the work was soon completed.

Grants were obtained to replace the windows in the OTC with double glazed units and new seating was installed in the lounge area, and the kitchen was refurbished. Farm paddocks were fenced and gates repaired or re-hung. In Hartford Wood the Cob cottage was repaired, the walls were rendered and a trench dug to divert water away from the building. Paths were improved, and Simon Sinkinson re-thatched the ridge of the roof to waterproof it.

It was decided that a board showing photographs of all staff should be put up in the foyer of the OTC so that visitors would be able to see who staff were and what jobs they did. This included David Bridges, Manager, with Rosalyn Reed and Jenny O'Dell on the admin team, Education Officers Alison Charters, Lucy Attwood and Angela Munn, assisted by Dan Kent and Kate Lee, Community Officer Vivien Drake and her assistant Fiona Harrower. In the OTC was Vivien Trollope, Gill Smart, Cathy Sherwood and Emma Shelley, and on the Farm Elaine Stawinoga (formerly Elaine Knight) and Nick Gill, leaving Chris Rogers on Maintenance, Ulrike Seydel in the Garden and Graham Bowring on cleaning duties at the NFSC. Visiting teachers and children really liked to see the pictures of the CET staff with whom they would come in contact and it was much easier for them to learn their names and know when strangers were on site.

For some time it had been realised that the seating area in the OTC was too small to comfortably accommodate residential groups so plans were drawn up to replace the existing structure with a new conservatory that would provide double the space. The work started in December and it was completed by early 2004 with improved seating constructed by Chris and replacement chairs and sofas.

Many efforts were made to raise money for the CET in 2003. Derek Rosling, one of the Trustees, encouraged local friends who gave a total of £24,000. Everyone was most grateful to them. Another initiative to raise money was by Dan Kent who ran in the London Marathon and managed to raise the magnificent sum of £800. This was followed by an impressive effort by Alex Glanville who cycled the 250 miles to Hautvillers in France raising over £3,000. This was a good destination as the town is twinned with Beaulieu.

There were more staff changes early in 2004. Anna Hanks replaced Angela Munn on the Education Team and Steve Barnard was appointed as Seasonal Education Officer to work the summer season. In the OTC Jill Gill transferred to join Elaine on the Farm when Nick left, and Jasmine Philpott and Judith Brown joined the team in the OTC. The CET also welcomed Dawid Krzeptowski from Poland on a European placement scheme.

The CET had enjoyed the status of Eco-Centre for three years and it was now time to renew that. Much extra work was needed to ensure that the Trust still warranted this status. Viv had worked very hard to encourage everyone to recycle and had brought in a number of measures to ensure that the CET was as 'green' as possible. One initiative was to introduce a 'Rocket' composter which would turn food waste into compost in just 6 weeks. It was installed and came into use in January. It was not without its teething problems but, in time, it was installed in a shed at the back of the garden and helped to deal with the cooked waste that had always been difficult to manage.

A lot of work had been done in the garden by this time. The glasshouse was in use, although the idea of producing food crops from around the world had proved difficult and expensive. David and Ulrike had spent a great deal of time and effort in re-planning the garden and had laid out vegetable beds, established a new herb garden and established production on organic principles. There was still much to do and Ralph Montagu asked Susan Campbell to prepare a report on the Garden to improve the impact and potential use.

The farm continued to be as popular as ever for visiting groups. Letters from children staying at the Out of Town Centre indicated that, although all aspects of their visit had been well received and exciting, for many children feeding the animals on the farm had been the highlight of their visit. They also loved to see hatching chicks. Some groups spent half a day on the farm as they had done in the early days of the OTC, others were only involved in the animal feeding morning and evening. This left time during the day to provide activities for Pre-schools and Little and Big Owl groups to come on half-day farm and garden visits. Totton Collage groups also started to come on a regular weekly basis during the term time. These were less able students or ones with special educational needs and the

experience of looking after the animals, cleaning them out, and doing many other jobs on the farm and in the garden helped them to gain confidence. In some cases it encouraged them to go on to further training at Sparsholt College in animal management or agriculture.

There was a really successful Open Day at the OTC in April 2004 with sheep and cows in the paddock, goats to be milked and tractors and machinery to be seen. There were also activities such as bread and butter making, and talks and demonstrations including hedgehog talks and spinning. Visitors stayed for several hours enjoying tea/coffee with cakes, etc, in the residential centre and a BBQ in the playfield, and children played on the adventure playground.

The community programme continued to offer an interesting range of courses including astronomy, plants, a marine course on the IOW, guided walks on the Beaulieu estate at Sowley, Exbury and Bucklers Hard, a moth evening, an organic gardening course and a charcoal earth burn that was a feature of the Open Day at the NFSC in July.

The CET had not attended the NF Show for a few years but a 10' x 10' pitch in the Countryside Area was offered free of charge and David accepted the offer. It was not a particularly good position within the area but the Countryside Area as a whole did win the President's Cup for 'best in show for education and demonstrating an awareness of country sports and pursuits to the general public, particularly children', so the CET made a positive contribution and it all raised awareness of the services of the CET.

In September 2004 Ulrike moved on to take up a teacher training position. Her contract was due to end in December as the 3 year grant finished then. She had found that she had a real interest in the teaching side of the garden work and was very good at it, so it seemed a good opportunity for her to advance her career. It did, however, leave a hole that needed to be filled. Steve Barnard finished his period as Seasonal Education Officer just then so he was appointed to work in the garden until the end of the year. Ros, who had helped a great deal with the garden before Ulrike was appointed, also renewed her interest in the garden while continuing as Trust Administrator.

Camping had been introduced on the site and had proved quite popular during weekend and summer holidays but it was not entirely without its problems. There were no staff on duty at weekends to check people in and out and no one to monitor or guide them, so they tended to wander all over the site. Self-catering groups objected to this, and it was not very satisfactory on the farm as the animals were vulnerable, and occasionally doors or gates were left open allowing them to escape. There were also complaints that the shower facility was poor and toilets were not cleaned. Much thought needed to be given to this before the new season started in 2005.

Towards the end of 2004 a second minibus was purchased. It was a fairly elderly item and was to replace the van that had served to move goods about the sites. At first it was felt that it might not be needed as a bus and that the seats could be taken out. However, it proved to be such a useful addition that staff soon wondered how they had ever managed with only one bus. Trips to take children to the start of the stream study and to transport them to Bucklers Hard or to the Forest could be done in half the time which gave the children opportunity for more field studies rather than waiting around for the rest of the class.

Volunteers have always been an enormous and essential help to the CET. The Trustees, of course, are all volunteers and have always done a marvellous job of guiding the work and overseeing the financial situation. Many volunteers have always helped with Open Days, and those could not be managed without them. Day to day activities such as help in the office, distributing publicity material, or help with maintenance are also invaluable. So it was with great sadness that staff learnt of the death of Roger Lushington who had served as a Trustee of the OTC in the early days, and as a volunteer and friend for many years. A sweet chestnut tree was planted in his memory near the car parks at the front. Another volunteer whose contribution was recognised was Rick Withers who had helped with maintenance, Open Days and a host of other activities for 20 years. He felt more like a member of staff than a volunteer. His help had been invaluable and he had even involved his son Glen from a very early age.

2005

2005 was the 30th Anniversary of the Trust so a year to celebrate. In February there was a 'Reception for Benefactors'. Trustees and staff welcomed those who had donated money or resources to the Trust in the past. It was also an important time to advise people of the need to replace the old buildings at the New Forest Study Centre and gain further support to fund the project. Grant money had been obtained to update the facilities allowing greater access for disabled visitors. This was particularly important on Open Days when the CET

hoped to encourage people from all parts of the community to enjoy all that was available on the sites. A 30th Anniversary Open Day was planned for the summer and no one was to be excluded.

Ros took responsibility for the garden when Steve Barnard left in December 2004. She had always been really interested in horticulture and had an RHS Advanced Certificate in Horticulture as well as a teaching certificate and a lifetime of gardening experience. There was no money to fund a gardening post so she started a weekly volunteer group who met each Tuesday morning and between them they managed to keep the garden in good order and continued to develop it. She remained Trust Administrator and worked in the office on other days.

Interesting things were happening at the NFSC. The children's rabbit tunnel in the wood was replaced by Chris as the old one had collapsed. Repairs were done to the cob cottage walls, and everything possible done to keep the old buildings in good order and usable by visiting groups until a replacement solution had been worked out. Viv Drake raised the funds and organised for the roundhouse to be replaced by participants on a course led by Jake Keen. The old one had been much used until it had collapsed over

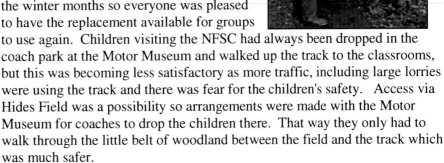

the winter months so everyone was pleased to have the replacement available for groups

to use again. Children visiting the NFSC had always been dropped in the coach park at the Motor Museum and walked up the track to the classrooms, but this was becoming less satisfactory as more traffic, including large lorries were using the track and there was fear for the children's safety. Access via Hides Field was a possibility so arrangements were made with the Motor Museum for coaches to drop the children there. That way they only had to walk through the little belt of woodland between the field and the track which was much safer.

New fleeces were ordered for staff, marked with the CET logo, which gave a more united and professional look. These were much appreciated by the staff and worn with pride.

The Estate/Countryside Day was another great success. Children followed two different trails through the wood and saw Beaulieu estate staff making fence posts, cutting timber into boards, using a chain saw to cut firewood and then processing it with a splitting machine. Other wood was turned into woodchip with another fascinating machine, and the game keeping staff gave interesting talks about their work. The historical theme continued as the children

learnt about life in Tudor times at the cob cottage and saw how items used to be produced using a pole lathe. They also learnt about commoning and were able to see and handle Mikey, the pony. The Estate Day had been making a big impact on children and their teachers for four years by that time.

The reception and Open Day to celebrate the 30th Anniversary went with a swing. It had a western theme and all staff dressed up in cowboy style costumes to add fun to the occasion. There was a VIP reception from 3 - 4 pm followed by a public Open Day and Barn Dance from 4.30 - 9 pm. Visitors could take part in activities as diverse as 'pistols at high noon', gold panning and throwing the horseshoe, to a toddler assault course, pony and trap rides and a fancy dress competition. There was food and dancing, beer and soft drinks and, of course, a celebratory cake. What a triumph for the CET to have been providing great quality countryside and environmental education to so many children and adults for 30 years; something well worth celebrating.

Activities continued with four weeks of holiday activities for children aged from 6 to 16 years, day visits on the farm and at the NFSC, residential courses and a host of community events. There was fundraising to be done and organised, plans to be worked out to replace the NFSC buildings and a host of other administrative tasks. An Open Day at the NFSC was organised in October. Also concern about the bird flu epidemic created much work in providing bio security measures on the farm. The Christmas Fair took place in November and the Victorian Christmas activities at Palace House for visiting school children were well attended again at the end of the Christmas Term. It had proved to be a very busy year for everyone.

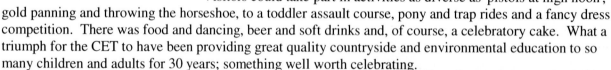

Everyone gave a sigh of relief and took a holiday over the Christmas period, but an incident on Christmas Eve caused great upset and concern. Someone crept into the farmyard at night and set fire to the barn where the hay and straw were stored. The whole barn was destroyed with all its contents. This was a big problem as animals still had to be fed and cared for. Fortunately, good friends helped out and the NFU quickly settled the insurance claim and Hants CC gave a grant of £5,000 towards greater security and extra expenses incurred in rebuilding, all of which was much appreciated. The barn at the CET was only the beginning of a sustained campaign by the arsonist who set fire to a number of farm buildings in the surrounding area and finally the Beaulieu Mill, a truly important historical building. The police worked

really hard to apprehend the culprit and everyone became really angry at this mindless and vindictive destruction.

David was very keen for the CET to work closely with other organisations in the New Forest area, particularly those providing education. A company called Liquid Logistics was offering corporate team building days and they were keen to co-operate and incorporate activities offered by the Trust to groups booked with them. Likewise they were willing for the CET to use their facilities for holiday activities. Closer working relations were soon built up to the benefit of all.

For a number of years there had been a large telescope set up in a small wooden observatory on the farm site. This belonged to Brian Sothcott, a keen amateur astronomer attached to Southampton University Astronomical Society. Several times each year he had brought groups to use the telescope, particularly when something significant could be seen in the night sky. However, it seemed very under-used and he wanted more groups to benefit from it. He began to offer the opportunity for residential groups to have talks with a chance to observe the night sky. He also started an astronomy club which allowed members access to the OTC site to use it. Several of his friends from the Astronomical Society profited from this for a time and used it on a regular basis. However, he became ill in later years and when he died he gave the telescope to the CET.

2006

By 2006 the annual Open Days had settled into a regular pattern with two at the OTC in April and July, and one in the autumn during the October half term at the NFSC, but in March 2006 the programme was enlivened by a quiz evening held at the Domus on the Motor Museum site. Freddie Rostand was persuaded to be Quizmaster and the Domus was packed to capacity so it was an evening of great fun and laughter.

David was kept very busy with activities and planning related to the rebuilding of the NFSC. There were also many visitors from those organising education for the National Parks Authority. An inspection by the

Fire Officer led to the installation of a new fire alarm system in the OTC and a great many time consuming improvements to the building. These were made far more difficult as Chris had a nasty fall early in the year, breaking his heel, and was off work while it mended. Once again the CET was much indebted to Rick who did much of the work required. There were a number of staff changes. Steve Barnard returned as a permanent Education Officer joining Alison Charters and Anna Hanks as the three education staff. John Jackman joined the staff as Farm Assistant, but later became Farmer when Elaine left in the autumn. She had worked on the farm for 26 years. When Gill left he was joined by Lisa van

Hennik. By this time, Ros had been giving more and more time to the garden, on Tuesdays and in her own time. When Jenny O'Dell decided to take early retirement, it seemed a good time to make Ros Garden Officer and replace her and Jenny with a full-time post of Administrator/PA. This position was taken by Lynda Hayward, later to become Lynda Leyman on her marriage to Mark. Donna Randell joined the OTC staff early in the year and when Dawid moved on, he was replaced by Liz Masebo. There was the usual turnaround of the three work placement positions in September so it really was a year of change.

By the end of the year the plans for the replacement of the NFSC had really gained momentum. An exciting plan to build a treehouse classroom had been proposed and accepted. This soon expanded to being 2 treehouses and an office/toilet block building with additional space for storage. In addition, a modern wood fuelled heating system was proposed to provide the necessary warmth. A fundraiser was appointed to help with putting the necessary finance in place and an ambitious scheme was implemented whereby architectural students could submit plans showing the design and layout of one of the treehouse buildings. This was run as a competition and the

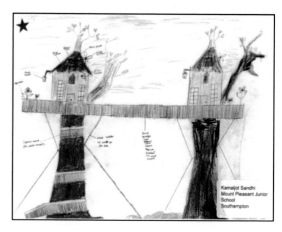

winning design would be built by the contractors, Blue Forest, as part of the complex. The student would also be awarded a year's work placement to be involved with the build. A number of local schools were also asked to run a competition for their children to draw treehouse designs. Both groups would be involved in Engagements Days when their work would be displayed at the Brabazon at the Motor Museum. The designs would then be judged and prizes awarded.

Finance, as always, was a big issue. Fortunately there was great interest and support from SEEDA (South East Educational Development Association) who offered half the money for the build. This meant that the CET had to raise the other half. The fundraiser, Isabel White, would certainly have her work cut out and she would need lots of help from David and Trustees if the required sum was to be obtained. One incredible effort to raise money was made by Viv Drake who undertook an 'Iron Man Challenge'. This involved 1.2 miles swimming, followed by a 56 mile cycle and then a 13 mile run, all to take place in Exmoor in March 2007. Much training had to be done and advertising of the event in order to maximise the fundraising opportunity. Well over £6,000 was raised.

There was still a great demand for Holiday Activities which were offered at Easter, in the Summer Holidays and the Autumn Half Term. Each of the courses was a masterpiece of invention and excitement devised by the Education staff on a wide range of topics. However, booking patterns had changed. In the 1980's there were only the Summer Holiday Activities and very little competition from other providers. As soon as they were advertised at the end of April there would be a deluge of applications for places. By 2006 there were far more opportunities for children during the school holidays and a much greater number of mothers who worked and had, of necessity, made other arrangements for the care of their children. This led to applications for places being made much later, even requests for places on the actual day of the activity. This made preparation difficult and a lot more advertising was required to ensure that places were filled.

2007

In January 2007 the CET started a new venture. Animals raised on the farm were to be slaughtered and butchered so that they could be sold directly from the OTC to the customers. These animals would have been raised in the happy, carefree environment of the CET farm, killed with the least possible stress, then packaged and frozen ready for sale. This proved very attractive to visitors and regular customers and ensured that the CET received a good return from all the work involved in rearing and caring for the animals.

The tractor on the farm had been causing serious concern for some time and it was decided that a Siromer flat pack tractor should be purchased. This would give an opportunity for the students from Totton College, who visited the farm each week, to take part in the assembly. John, Lisa, Chris and Rick helped the students and they worked with a will, succeeding in just a few weeks to produce a fully working tractor. They learnt an enormous amount from this exercise and were absolutely delighted to see 'their tractor' being regularly used for the ongoing farm work.

After the disasterous fire of Christmas 2005, the farm staff were pleased to announce in March that the new barn had been completed. This was half as big again as the old one had been, so much more useful for storing all that was need. Perhaps bad things can give good results after all.

With Ros now fully employed in the garden, the time had come to offer children staying at the OTC the opportunity of a session in the garden each morning. A group of 6 - 10 children would go out each day in the same way that they went out to do animal

feeding. This was immediately popular, and it was soon apparent that the children had very little knowledge of gardening. They were introduced to planting seeds and potatoes as appropriate, harvesting vegetables, herbs and fruit and taking part in as many other activities as the limited time allowed.

It was a big shock one morning in February to find a very large oak tree had fallen across the herb garden during the night. The top branches were only about 6 feet from the

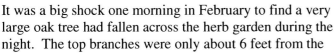

OTC residential building so it could have been very serious indeed. The children soon helped Ros to start the clear up in their morning session so at least access to the garden could be achieved, but Wessex Tree Surgeons had to come and remove the bulk of it. Fortunately, the tree fell from a neighbours garden so organising the removal and the insurance claim did not have to be done by CET staff, but there was considerable work needed to restore the herb garden to some sort of order.

The Community Programme was really interesting for the year. A lecture by Aubrey Manning took place in March, followed by a Dawn Chorus Walk in May. There was another quiz night with Esther Ransom asking the questions and David Bellamy gave an interesting talk in the autumn. Paul Manning provided falconry courses and Bob Mizen helped people to understand astronomy. There was also a great barn dance to celebrate the official opening of the new barn. The local fire brigade added some fun with a shower of water to remind everyone of their part in dousing the flames.

These were in addition to all the usual Open Days, holiday activities, Big Owls and Little Owls, walks, talks and courses that were a regular feature each year.

In June everyone who had taken part in building the cob cottage in Hartford Wood was invited to a party to mark the 10th Anniversary of its construction. This included an opportunity for repairs to be made to the building. Cob cottages must always have needed constant upkeep and repair. Those living in them in the past would have been on site and able to do remedial work as the need arose, but for the 'House in Time', jobs had to be planned and executed by staff and volunteers. So it was really good to have a committed team of volunteers willing to help with repairs to the walls, thatch and woodwork, to mend or replace broken furniture, rebuild the front fence and clear encroaching vegetation. A BBQ and a chance to catch up on news made it a very enjoyable occasion.

The demanding job of raising funds for the new Treehouse Study Centre continued throughout the year and David was kept very busy on the project. Planning permission had been granted, Hampshire CC were supporting the project with a grant of £100,000, and SEEDA had promised £250,000 so everything was moving on well. Samantha Sherwood had submitted the winning design and was delighted to know that the build would soon start. There were many questions to be answered, of course, such as: how would groups be managed during the build; what toilet facilities would be provided; where would everything be stored; and many others.

While all this was happening a real effort had to be made to keep all services going as usual. Terri Parkinson and Caroline Staines joined the staff in the OTC as others left. Visiting groups came and went and still had to be catered for in the OTC. Animals were born on the farm, and turkeys arrived to be raised for the Christmas market. Vegetables were produced in great number and a new market had to be found in the summer holiday period when there were no groups needing them in the OTC. So the busy life of the Trust continued as usual with all its challenges, delights and concerns.

Another project that began in the garden in 2007 was the construction of a Sensory Garden. It was an ambitious project as it required alterations to a raised garden, a new paved path, and a circular area in the centre that was to be a mosaic. This would be a really eye-catching feature and would have to be done with great care and precision. Volunteers helped with all the ground works and then the time came to finalise the plans for the mosaic. Ros had not done anything like that before so she went on a course to learn how it should be done. Her tutor, Oliver Budd, was most helpful and took a real interest in the project. Schools were invited to encourage their pupils to submit ideas for the mosaic and also for the planting and features for the sensory garden. Some really good entries were submitted and those who gave the best ideas were invited to come, with their classes or school clubs, to help construct it and do the planting. Four groups came and had wonderful days doing the

work. None of it would have been possible without the help of volunteers and one of the placement students, Michaela Zweimuller. The mosaic really added to the feature as it would be bright and colourful throughout the year.

Sadly, in November 2007 Graham Carter died. He was the first Director of the Trust, and had done so much to develop the whole work throughout the 28 years he was in office. He inspired, guided, encouraged and even fought for its very survival in the many difficult times it faced. His vision was truly international and his commitment unlimited. His motto of 'think globally, act locally' encouraged staff to give education the highest possible value and the development of each child and adult was of greatest importance to him. It was a very sad day for all those who had worked for him or had contact with him over the years.

71

Building the Treehouse Study Centre - 2008

In December 2007 the great construction of the new Treehouse Study Centre began. Much work had been done by CET staff to prepare for the work to start. A marquee was put up and the education staff went through all the teaching materials, equipment and junk that had accumulated over the 27 years since the first building had been erected in Hartford Wood in 1980. No doubt some of this had been done over the years, but it was amazing how much had been kept 'in case it might come in useful'. Then Chris and Rick salvaged all the materials from the old buildings that could possibly be put to other uses. Nothing should be wasted. When the contractors arrived most of the site clearance work had been completed.

The first task in the construction was to create the great many concrete pads on which the timbers to support the structure would be placed. It always takes a while to established the foundations of any building, but soon the structure was rising from the ground and it was clear that these were going to be really impressive buildings. It was a really demanding task to keep the project on track and ensure that costs did not spiral out of control. Blue Forest had a fixed price contract, but even so, things could go wrong and extra costs could be incurred. David had to be constantly vigilant and it took a great deal of his time and energy to supervise the work. The whole building was designed to be as eco-friendly as possible: the sourcing of materials, providing solar and PV panels, harvesting rainwater, the insulation and many other features. It was a truly award winning design.

Treehouse One was officially handed over to the Trust in July and was put to use straight away. The children were so excited to see the building for the first time. The light airy classroom gave a great feeling of space, and as they climbed to the top of the tower they could look out into the tree canopy and really feel as if they were in the top of the trees. Then they could go out onto the terrace, raised some twenty feet off the ground, and be lords of all they surveyed. There would certainly be many uses for this lovely building in the future.

However, there was still much to do to complete the other buildings before the official opening on 25th September, but the Blue Forest staff worked hard and, by opening day, everything was in place to make it a very memorable occasion. Alan Titchmarsh arrived with all the invited guests and after a short speech officially declared the 'New Forest Treehouse Study Centre' open for business. Food and drinks were served and the buildings explored. The connecting swinging bridge was investigated and enjoyed and there was a real festive atmosphere to the day. The completed buildings certainly had an enormous presence and were much admired by Benefactors, Friends and Trustees and the many visitors who attended. Treehouse One was named the 'Beaulieu Beaufort Foundation Treehouse' as that organisation had given enormous financial support and, in recognition of the great contribution Graham had made to the CET, Treehouse Two was named the 'Graham Carter Treehouse'. He would have been delighted.

Early in 2008 the CET was approached by Derek Olden of the National Vintage Tractor and Engine Club. The members of the Club had always had a summer get-together and open weekend in the area, but their former venue was no longer available to them and they needed a new site. It was agreed that a joint open event with the CET would be a good opportunity for both organisations, so a Country Fair was planned for 13th/14th July. Unfortunately the best laid plans can easily be ruined by the weather. The ground was totally waterlogged and the whole weekend had to be cancelled.

There was also a project to improve the herb garden that year. All the rain had turned it into a pond that the ducks soon discovered and enjoyed. However, the Mediterranean herbs were not at all happy and most of them died. Viv Drake had a friend, Angus White, who was the Manager of Ruscrete at Totton, and he was a great help in providing wooden sleepers and soil to create a raised garden. He even encouraged someone to help with the build. Drainage pipes were put in and when all was completed, Patrick Fairweather supplied a range of herbs to make it a very attractive feature in the centre of the garden.

The Christmas Fair had always been a most significant fundraising event each year, but it was getting very crowded on the Friday and there were many Friends of the Trust who were unable to be there during the day. So the fundraising committee decided to have a gala pre-view on the Thursday evening to which guests would be invited. This was a great success and in no way diminished the impact of the Fair itself on the following day, so it was decided that it should become an annual event.

Christmas and New Year came and went and 2009 began. A big effort was made to keep the birds fed in the Garden. A feeding station was set up in the bushes just outside the Garden Room where a great range of birds could be watched from inside. The most numerous were the tits with blue, great, coal, long tailed and willow tits hanging from the feeders. Then sparrows, chaffinches, blackbirds and the odd thrush came and picked up the seeds beneath or visited the bird table. There were the more occasional nuthatches, great spotted and green woodpeckers to be seen, while pheasants and pigeons became quite persistent and would devour anything available at great speed. It was fascinating to watch.

Staff of the CET have always tried to take part in local events, despite their very busy schedules, and Shrove Tuesday was no exception. The Beaulieu Village School had planned to have a Pancake Day and all local organisations were asked to take part. Races were held between groups amid much fun and laughter. Pancakes were tossed, and dropped, while the High Street was closed to traffic and the whole occasion reflected the

community involvement that would have been seen in villages in the past. It was great fun for the children and gave them a real flavour of our historic traditions.

In June Karen Bennie joined the staff. She was sponsored by the John Lewis Partnership and was on a six month placement with the CET. She was able to help in all areas of the Trust and proved to be a great enthusiast for all aspects of the work. She arranged for a number of donations of furniture, soft furnishings and bedding to be made by John Lewis, and their staff were encouraged to take part in a big redecorating project within the residential centre. Their input was certainly a great asset to the Trust.

2009 - 2010

A field kitchen was constructed in 2009. It was a round-wood construction with metal roof, and positioned at the far end of the Garden. Inside a mud oven was constructed that would allow for cooking demonstrations and courses, as well as providing an opportunity for people to make pizzas on Open Days. The first chance for this to happen was on the big Open Day held on 15th & 16th August. This was a joint venture with the Vintage Tractor and Engine Club similar to the one planned in 2008, but there was more success with the weather and the day was a great success. There was a terrific range of old vehicles and engines for people to see, including parades of vehicles in an arena set up in the field above the orchard.

There were also stalls with interesting vehicle related items on sale. On the lower part of the OTC site there were farm activities, craft stalls and displays including pole lathe demonstrations and bee keeping. Special trails and activities were provided for the children and refreshments and BBQ food could be purchased from the OTC and playfield. This was greatly appreciated by the visitors.

The driving of minibuses was proving a problem as younger staff did not have the necessary D1 qualification on their driving licences. Anyone taking their driving test after 1997 was not automatically allowed to drive a minibus and had to take a further qualification to do so. The course to obtain this cost nearly £1000 per person, so it was not practical for the CET to put staff through the training. It was therefore decided that a nine seater minibus would be purchased that could be driven by anyone with a driving licence. This helped to alleviate the problem, but drivers with a qualification to drive a 17 seat minibus were still needed for trips to Bucklers Hard, etc. Many schools were having similar problems in providing drivers for school activities.

Work was carried out on the Farm to replace the sheds for the laying hens. This work was supported by John Lewis again. They really were a great help. The new sheds would provide nest boxes accessible from the outside so that the eggs could be collected more easily, and they would give more room for the hens with easy access to their outside pens. All the work was done in-house by Chris, Rick and John.

One of the conditions of planning permission for the building of the Treehouses was that a fence be erected to enclose the site. No doubt it was a health and safety issue as anyone falling from the walkways or Treehouse buildings could be badly hurt. It would also increase security. It was decided that a deer fence, erected to enclose not only the buildings but the whole area that was actively managed by the CET, would be the best solution. This would mean that the Cob Cottage was included within the fence and all the areas that were in the coppice rotation. There had been some concern earlier that someone had been using the Cob Cottage as sleeping accommodation. A fire had been lit and furniture moved around in the absence of CET staff. Perhaps the fence would help to deter that activity. Also deer are a real problem in an area of coppice as they graze the new shoots, prevent the coppice stool from re-growing properly or even kill it. The fencing was carried out by members of the NFCV (New Forest Conservation Volunteers) under the guidance of Hugh Corrie. They had done a lot of maintenance and conservation work for the Trust over the years, which had been much appreciated.

In the summer the CET was invited to take part in the New Forest Show again in the Forest Food Area. It was suggested that the CET provided a display of poultry, some educational input and a display of vegetables. There are so many wonderful stands at the NF Show that it is always a challenge to provide something really striking, but all staff worked hard to contribute. The final effort included live turkeys in a poultry arc, quizzes and puzzles for both adults and children, and a display of vegetables and flowers that had been grown in pots in the Garden. The Forest Food Area was voted 'Best in Show' so everyone felt that they had contributed to that success.

There were some staff changes in Sept 2010. Viv Drake, who had worked for the Trust for 22 years, became a freelance consultant to the Trust. She would still prepare the activities for the Community Programme on a contract basis and attend courses as necessary. She would also put in applications for grants and help at Open Days. These new arrangements would enable her to take work from other organisations and she would work from home. Lucy Hale, who had been one of the Education Officers, full time at first, and part time after her children were born, and finally caretaker/cleaner at the Treehouse, also moved on at that time.

The Summer Holiday Activities were a great success again and included a new activity called 'Barnstorming'. This gave children an opportunity to take part in work and games on the Farm. Many of them had little or no experience of animals or farming and John and Lisa did a great job of encouraging and teaching them, and giving them a really good time.

The Recession by this time, which began in 2008, was having a really bad effect on the finances of the Trust. Grants were difficult to obtain and those from Local Authorities had been cut. Schools were cutting back on residential and day trips and even those that were booked were often staying for shorter periods or with less children. Every effort was being made by David, the Fundraising Committee and Trustees to help boost income, but staff were continually reminded not to spend any money. Even necessary materials for maintenance were severely restricted and times were hard. Some grants were received, however, one of which was from the Sustainable Development Fund to replace the solar heating for

the residential centre and install air to air heat pumps for the OTC, offices and Garden Room. The heat pumps would not only improve the heating in the buildings, but would also reduce costs.

The CET continued to provide courses for those with special needs. This had become a really important part of the work of the Trust. Groups with disabilities and special educational needs from Totton College had been using the OTC for three days each week for a number of years. People with mental illnesses, from MIND, had helped in the Garden and on the Farm, and children from schools with high numbers of children from

poorer homes had experienced residential weeks paid for by grants from the lottery and businesses. In addition, young people from main stream schools and special schools had benefitted from periods of work experience supervised by CET staff.

2011 - 2012

2011 was a year of changes in staffing. At the beginning of the year there had to be some reorganisation of staff. With no Community Officer now on site the extra work had to be undertaken by the Education Officers. Anna was promoted to Education and Development Officer. This gave her a much wider role as well as now leading the education staff who would be responsible for more planning of courses, presenting Little and Big Owls and supervising and organising the tasks of all the work placement staff. Alison Charters, now Alison Bath since her marriage the previous year, announced that she was pregnant and expecting a baby in May. A little girl, Emma, was actually born in April and Will Burns became Education Officer to cover Alison's maternity leave. Lynda Leyman became PA/Office Manager with increased responsibilities.

Another change was that Ros had decided that she would like to reduce her hours and work only 3 days per week. An Assistant Gardener was appointed in February to also work 3 days per week so there was one day overlap when the work was co-ordinated, and the whole week was covered. Both Ros and her assistant, Steve Andrew, worked shorter days so it had the effect of saving the Trust money at the same time as providing extra teaching cover for residential groups taking part in the morning gardening routine. This worked well throughout the year but in December after 24 years with the Trust, Ros retired promising to come back as a volunteer in the new year.

The Farm and residential centre also experienced changes. John Jackman left and was replaced by Eric Dovey. Lisa did a wonderful job in covering the work and keeping all the animals healthy in between. Viv Trollope also left the staff of the Out of Town Centre after over 30 years. Terri Parkinson then took charge of the kitchen assisted by Jane Wainwright, while Donna became Housekeeping Co-ordinator with Sharon Bowness as Domestic Assistant. There were the usual changes to the work placement positions in September, so there really was never a dull moment.

Fundraising continued to be a big issue and both Jan Hoy and the fundraising committee continued to do an amazing job. A wonderful range of events were staged by each of them culminating in a magnificent Christmas Fair. They all deserved a very big 'Thank you' for all their hard work.

There was always maintenance work to be done in the wood and it was decided to start a group of Conservation Volunteers who would meet once a month to do tasks such as relaying paths, repairing bridges, cleaning out ponds, doing a butterfly survey and many other activities. A small group started, soon joined by employees of Southern Electric. There was a system within Southern Electric where each staff member was allowed 3 paid days each year when they could go and work for a charity of their choice and the CET was one of the organisations that they recommended. Six of their staff came each month and enjoyed it so much that several of them would negotiate to get extra days when other members of Southern Electric staff didn't want to take their quota of volunteer days. Of course, there was always a limit to how many times they could do that, but it became quite a fun activity for some of them to see how many days they could get to spend in the wood.

At the end of the year the turkeys were processed as usual. Many happy customers enjoyed them for their Christmas dinners and staff were pleased to see all the work completed. It was a very demanding job to raise almost 70 birds then kill, draw and prepare them for sale for the festive season each year, but many of the staff and volunteers took part at the end and there was a real party atmosphere as the autumn term drew to a close.

The farm received a replacement tractor in 2012. The old blue Ford tractor given to the CET in 1980 had really served very well, but all good things come to an end. Unfortunately, despite a grant of £2,500 from Hants CC there was not much money in the coffers and Eric had to look around for the best he could get for the money. Tractors are expensive items, so once again it had to be very second hand. Three lambs were born in January, followed by piglets, baby goats, ducklings and chicks. What a lovely time to be on a farm and see all this new life.

The Woodland Trust had been offering trees for hedges that would provide fruits and nuts for wildlife, so David had applied for some and they were planted both at the OTC and the woodland site. Another tree fell on the Garden in February. Unfortunately it hit the greenhouse and, although it could have been much worse, it did cause quite a lot of damage and disruption. The shards of glass were like daggers and would have caused serious injury to anyone in the greenhouse at the time, but it happened overnight so that danger was averted. It took several weeks to clear up the mess, and for insurance money to be paid.

A new venture for the CET was to hold weddings at the Treehouse. This was very much in the spirit of the Trust's Deed as it gave the opportunity to welcome other groups of people to enjoy the countryside. Twelve weddings per year would be possible, and these would make a significant contribution to the finances. Keeping the books balanced was still a real problem so any additional funds were more than welcome.

Ben and Snowflake, two New Forest ponies owned by the Trust, were pressed into service to help with a new Holiday Activity on the farm. Lisa spent a lot of time schooling them so that they could be ridden by the children who took part in an activity called 'Own a Pony'. This was a delightful course that gave the children an opportunity to groom, tack up and ride the two ponies. It was so popular that an additional day had to be included to meet demand. Ben and Snowflake behaved beautifully and continued to take part in Open Days thereafter giving rides to children throughout the days.

During the year there were again staff changes, but fortunately, not so many as in 2011. Terri and her husband, also Terry, decided to move to Hungary to join Terry's sister. Janine took over in the kitchen. Alison returned from maternity leave, as Will's contract came to an end. Chris Rogers had been sick for long time and required a liver transplant so Rick, a volunteer to the Trust for many years, agreed to take his place for one day each week. Finally, at the end of the year, Eric resigned and Will Burns was appointed as Farmer.

2013

2013 was a worrying year. Finance was still a big problem. Hampshire County Council was the only Local Authority still supporting the CET and they had advised that their grant would be coming to an end. In future the Trust was going to have to be self-sufficient financially for all every day expenses and only look for grants for development projects. With that in mind new ventures were essential. Already the weddings established at the

Treehouse. were proving popular and future bookings looked good.

Another new venture was to provide more camping in the orchard at the OTC. This was no longer going to be done in-house as the work and supervision required was too much for the existing CET staff, so an arrangement was made that Eco-camping would pay a sum each year to the Trust and they would then organise the venture. A cabin was set up just outside the main office door to act as the reception point for campers and a shower block installed close to the outside toilets. The track through the middle of the farm, that led up the slope to the orchard, was upgraded.

Fire pits were set up to provide 40 pitches with places to light camp fires safely The whole enterprise was set up for 60 days camping between March and October to take place in weekends and school holidays when the Centre would not be in use for visiting school groups or Brownies. Despite poor weather early in the year, the OTC proved to be a very popular campsite, close to Beaulieu with all its attractions, in the New Forest and on a site truly different from anything else on offer and with plenty of outdoor activities available in the immediate area.

Archery had become popular both for people booking direct with the CET and for those booking through New Forest Activities, so it was decided to make a more permanent range available at the OTC. The local archery club was equally enthusiastic and very willing to help with setting it up. They also helped with installing a field archery course in Hartford Wood and both these new facilities were soon in use.

The falconry courses, set up by Paul and Mandy Manning, were continuing to be booked regularly. Their wonderful birds of prey were fascinating to visitors whether they were taking part in the courses or just had the opportunity to see them on their perches placed on the grass near the car park.

Clearly all these ventures were going to give a whole new meaning to 'access to the countryside'. Hopefully all these visitors would learn to love and value the countryside more as they took part in them.

2014

The three Open Days each year were well established by 2013 and continued in 2014. The one in April offered a Farm and Garden experience, and in the summer a two-day Countryside Show in partnership with the Vintage Tractor and Engine Club. There were lambs to be enjoyed in the spring, goats to be milked and eggs for sale, as well as all the usual animals, poultry and

machinery at both events. There were themed childrens' activities including farm and garden trails, planting seeds and seedlings and all the delights of the Garden to be enjoyed. There was pizza making in the mud ovens and displays that told about hedgehogs and bees, with craft demonstrations, falconry and Fontiersmen. Ben and Snowflake gave pony rides and, in the summer, there was a really good display of vintage tractors,

stationery engines and working machinery. The third Open Day was at the Treehouse in October. Visitors loved being in the woodland environment and experiencing activities such as a deer trail, 'earth magic walks', mole walks, orienteering and pond dipping. There was campfire cooking and storytelling, and an opportunity to visit the cob cottage nestled in a clearing in the wood. Pole lathe turning, chainsaw carving and log splitting took place near the treehouses where refreshments and BBQ food were served. All the Open Days were well attended and much enjoyed by all, and were a real opportunity for visitors to appreciate the wide range of activities offered by the CET throughout the year.

There were more staff changes. New babies were born to Anna and Lisa both of whom took maternity leave and they were covered by temporary staff in their absence. Simon Hemsley became full-time Garden Education Officer. Although it was sometimes hard to initiate new members of staff into the complicated working of the Trust, and there were some steep learning curves as they assimilated all that each job entailed, it always brought new ideas and enthusiasm, and a different range of skills and knowledge to the Trust. There was never the chance for the organisation to become dull or boring.

As 2014 dawned the Countryside Education Trust entered its 40th year as a registered charity, and it was an opportunity for Trustees, staff and long-term volunteers to take stock and consider the future of the organisation. In January Ralph Montagu, as chair of the Trustees, set up a Strategy Day to look at the current position of the Trust, what threats there were to the ongoing work and how it could take advantage of all the opportunities to consolidate and expand its programme. The Education staff clearly outlined what the CET was offering. Then there were a number of speakers on Outdoor Education, Learning through Landscapes, New Forest Activities and the Fortune Centre of Riding Therapy. The day finished by setting a number of objectives that would be supported by both Trustees and staff.

Hampshire County Council was still supporting the Trust at that time, but with Government cuts continuing it was decided that it could no longer do so. This led to many difficult decisions for the CET. After much heart searching and debate the Trustees decided that they would have to make David Bridges redundant. So after over 13 years with the Trust, David left in September. Jane Cooper, daughter of Graham Carter, who had been a Trustee for several years, agreed to become Executive Trustee. With her strategic and fundraising background, she had the skills required for the next stage of its development. Jane appointed Anna as Education Manager across the sites. The Trustees also made the decision to consolidate the Countryside Education Trust brand by removing the Out of Town Centre name, thus closing a chapter of the CET's history.

As the CET ended 2014 , there were still many challenges to face and exciting opportunities to embrace. Open Days continued to be planned, new educational programmes were devised for visitors young and old that would educate, thrill and inspire. Everyone involved looked forward to celebrating the Trust's 40th Birthday in May 2015 and the next 40 years of innovative, exciting and creative Countryside Education.

Summary

Educational Activities
at the Countryside Education Trust

On the Farm - Both children and adults love to see and handle the farm animals. They can also feed them, collect eggs, and milk the goats, all the time learning about where our food comes from and how it is produced.

In the Garden - Seeds can be sown and produce harvested. There are courses that teach how to grow vegetables, fruit, flowers and herbs and food produced in the garden can even be cooked in the field kitchen.

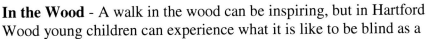

In the Wood - A walk in the wood can be inspiring, but in Hartford Wood young children can experience what it is like to be blind as a mole underground, how hard it is for a squirrel to balance on a branch, or how it feels to creep down a rabbit hole. Older children can learn about minibeasts, or animal homes and how they prepare for the winter, how animals interact with each other, their life cycles and who are the predators and who are the prey. The woodland offers many other opportunities for both children and adults to learn about woodland management, how trees grow, and identification of birds, flowers and fungi.

Fresh Water Studies - within the wood is a stream that rises on the heath above, and flows right down into the Beaulieu Estuary. On its way it passes through fish ladders, once used to raise trout, and a number of ponds. Students of all ages can learn and see for themselves how streams begin, how they are used, how fast they flow and how they meander from side to side. It is really exciting to discover what lives in the ponds from tiny freshwater shrimps, to whirligig beetles and the different species of newts.

Orienteering, Woodland Crafts and Archery - There are many opportunities to learn something different. Following a map is not always easy, but an orienteering course can be a big help. Woodland crafts can include making a hurdle or a besom broom, carving a spoon or learning to use a pole lathe. There could also be courses on spinning and weaving, or the chance to paint in the wood. A bow and arrow could provide a chance to shoot at a target or even to have a go at field archery.

All the Attractions of Beaulieu and Bucklers Hard - Based on the Beaulieu Estate, the CET has access to all the wonderful facilities there. The Motor Museum, Palace House and Beaulieu Abbey offer topics covering many historical themes from the life of a monk, to Victorians and the history of motoring, while Bucklers Hard highlights features of the shipbuilding industry. On the wider estate there is evidence of a lively brickmaking industry as well as the current activities of farming and forestry, plus Beaulieu village which is a study in itself.

On the Heathland and in the New Forest - There is so much to learn about the different habitats of the wood and heath land of the New Forest which is so close at hand for the CET. It is such a special place with its rare species and unique way of life.

Beach and Seashore - The beach at Lepe is just a short distance away and provides much interest from rock pooling to coastal erosion, while the nature reserve at Need's Ore provides opportunities to study migrating birds and further seashore activities.

Anyone booking for either a day or residential course with the Countryside Education Trust can be sure of a wonderful time that is both interesting and enlightening. Also those taking part in a holiday activity, a wedding or a birthday party will have a unique and exciting experience that they will remember for many years to come.

To contact the CET: Tel 01590 612401 or email: mail@cet.org.uk or visit on line www.cet.org.uk